IBM PCs and Compatibles

IBM PCs
AND COMPATIBLES
A Business User's Guide

COLIN LEWIS

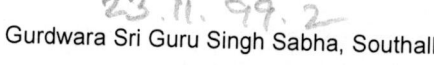

Basil Blackwell

First published 1986
Basil Blackwell Ltd
108 Cowley Road, Oxford OX4 1JF, UK

Basil Blackwell Inc.
432 Park Avenue South, Suite 1503,
New York, NY 10016, USA

British Library Cataloguing in Publication Data

Lewis, C.D.
    IBM PCs and compatibles: a business user's guide.
    1. IBM Personal Computer—Programming
    2. Business—Data processing
    I. Title
    658'.054165   HF5548.4.I24

    ISBN 0-631-14776-4

Library of Congress Cataloging in Publication Data

Lewis, Colin, 1938-
IBM PCs and compatibles.

Includes index.
1. IBM Personal Computer—Programming.   2. Business
—Data processing. I. Title.
HF5548.4.I24L49 1986   004.165   85–30792
ISBN 0-631-14776-4

Typeset by Columns of Reading
Printed in Great Britain.

In memory of our son Mark

Contents

Foreword — xi

1 IBM compatibles — 1
The role of IBM PCs in the microcomputer
  market-place — 1
The IBM PC family and its nearest rivals — 3
The IBM compatibles, clones and look-alikes — 6
Conclusion — 16

2 The operating systems PC–DOS/MS–DOS — 17
Operating systems — 17
Basic microcomputer configuration — 18
DOS — 19
Creating a National DOS disk — 23
DOS commands — 31
Creating an AUTOEXEC.BAT file — 45
Conclusion — 47
Summary of DOS commands — 47

3 Word processing packages — 51
General concept of word processing — 51
Editing and presentation facilities — 54
Control or organizational facilities — 58
Conclusion — 64
Review of the more popular word processing
  packages — 65

4 Spreadsheet packages including graphics — 68
The basic idea behind the spreadsheet concept — 69
Use of formulae and their replication — 70

Built-in functions   73
Examples of spreadsheets   75
Graphics   82
Colour   84
Macroprogramming   85
Iteration control and forward referencing   85
Simple database facilities   86
Conclusion   86
Review of the more popular spreadsheet
    packages   86

5 **Flexible database packages**   89
Database terminology   91
Classification of database packages   92
Designing the record structure and/or layout   94
Password access   98
Sorting and indexing   98
Searching for specified records   101
Report writing   104
Other facilities   109
Conclusion   115
Review of the more popular flexible database
    packages   116

6 **Integrated business packages**   119
The concept of integration – advantages and
    disadvantages   119
Integration from a user's point of view   122
Disk based and RAM based integrated business
    packages   123
Conclusion   128
Review of the more popular integrated business
    packages   129

7 **The microcomputer as a communications device** 133
Micro to micro communications – Local Area
    Networks   133
Micro to mainframe communications   137
General dial-up systems in the UK   139
Specialized dial-up database systems   143

Conclusion   145
Review of the more popular dial-up databases   146

Index   151

Foreword

This book is for the typical manager or business user of microcomputers. It describes how, in practical terms, he or she can make most effective use of the most commonly available packages on the most commonly available business microcomputer which, today, has to be an IBM PC or compatible. The book is intended as a digest of the essential facts required to achieve this aim, gathered from the myriad of manuals in which this information is hidden and camouflaged by material really only required by the professional programmer.

For those of us who have not only taken part in but have been interested observers of the growth in the use of microcomputers, the arrival of the IBM PC in the US in 1982, and subsequently in the UK in early 1983, at long last created a move towards a standard operating system and floppy disk format. Prior to this there had been a tentative move towards a common operating system for 8-bit business machines, namely CP/M, but even machines with this operating system invariably required a different disk format. There had been more than 16 for 5.25 inch disks alone.

With the advent of 16-bit machines and the arrival of the IBM PC with its operating system PC–DOS the majority of non-IBM computer manufacturers accepted that this was to be the *de facto* industry standard for single user, non-multi-tasking machines and started to produce micro-computers referred to as IBM compatibles using the operating system MS–DOS. The latter was to all intents and purposes the same as PC–DOS as both were produced by the software company Microsoft and they are therefore sometimes referred to collectively as PC/MS–DOS.

Whilst a microcomputer's operating system, which is essentially a collection of programs which organize and control the operation of the computer, is mainly of interest to programmers developing software for the machine, a limited knowledge of certain of the facilities offered by the operating system is required by any user wishing to use the microcomputer effectively. The problem, however, is that DOS manuals usually describe all the 50-odd programs and functions offered by the operating system and do not discriminate between those required by the programmer and those few but essential facilities required by a user only interested in using the computer as a management or business tool.

This book concentrates on those facilities of PC/MS–DOS required only by the latter.

A discussion of the facilities required of the operating system to operate a microcomputer installation effectively is followed by an examination of the principal types of application packages used by managers and business users, namely:

word processing packages,

spreadsheet packages,

flexible database packages,

integrated packages; and, in addition,

the microcomputer as a communications device.

In 1983, at the time of the UK launch of the IBM PC, there were only 50 dealers and 30 application packages; by 1985 there were 1,900 dealers and 5,500 packages. It is only possible in a book of this type, however, to cover the general principles and concepts which are available in the above packages and which are of particular use in management and business. The most widely used packages in each of these application areas are reviewed to give an idea of their relative advantages and disadvantages.

My main hope in writing this book is that, by synthesizing the many hours I have spent setting up application packages together with illustrative example files in an IBM PC or compatible based workshop, I will save the reader many frustrating hours in similar pursuit and allow him or her to concentrate on using an IBM PC or compatible simply as a management or business tool.

Colin Lewis

1

IBM compatibles

The role of IBM PCs in the microcomputer market-place

The introduction in the US in 1982, and subsequently in the UK during 1983, of the IBM PC (Personal Computer) brought about a long awaited rationalization of the microcomputer market-place. In the early days of micro-computers, that is, in the late 1970s, the microcomputer market consisted principally of Commodore Pets, Tandy machines and Apples. All these microcomputers had their own unique operating systems (usually built into the machine in ROM – read only memory) and unique disk formatting procedures. Subsequently, with the introduc-tion of disk based operating systems (as opposed to ROM based systems), a certain degree of standardization occurred since the operating system CP/M tended to dominate as the principal operating system for the then mainly 8-bit machines. However, even though it was then possible for an individual to move between machines without having to relearn a whole new set of operating instructions, it certainly was not possible to move infor-mation in the form of files held on floppy disks between machines simply because of the multitude of different disk formats that existed.

Thus in the early 1980s it appeared to the user that microcomputer manufacturers were basically in the business of 'non-compatibility', that is, they produced machines that could only exchange information with machines from the same manufacturing source. This situation may have been seen as one of simple self-interest on the part of the microcomputer manufacturers of the day but it can also be put down to the fact that in those early days of microcomputing virtually all manufacturers were companies that had grown from small beginnings and none was large enough to force the others to follow its standard since each presumed, or hoped, that its own would become the standard.

At about this time, it became evident to observant market watchers that the rate of growth of sales of large, mainframe computers was starting to decline since most large companies and organizations that could justify such large machines already had them. The future market-place for such large machines was to become one principally of replacement and enhancement rather than of original purchase. Thus for the first time the large computer manufacturers, who had tended to 'look down' on microcomputers as at worst toys for use at home and at best upgraded programmable calculators, began to realize that the microcomputer market had far more growth potential than the market for mainframe machines. Hence, the 'big boys' of the computer world – and in particular IBM – decided to muscle in on a market which had hitherto been mainly controlled by relatively small companies.

IBM's first move into the market was the instruction of the standard PC. Initial reviews of this 16-bit machine from the 'experts' were not very enthusiastic and indeed in retrospect it cannot be said that the IBM PC represented a breakthrough in microcomputer technology. In spite of the criticisms, however, the IBM PC very rapidly gained for itself a major portion of the international microcomputer market for business machines and it became evident to competitors that the reason for its success was not its technical specification but simply the fact that it at long last represented a standard, and that this was evidently what the market had been waiting for.

Thus, the name of the game for IBM's competitors in the microcomputer market became that of producing IBM 'compatibles', 'clones' or 'look alikes' which, without contravening IBM's copyright, provided a machine which did all that an IBM PC did but did it:

faster,

cheaper,

with free (or bundled) software,

with more storage for the same price,

with better keyboards, video displays, etc.

Technically it has not proved difficult to produce an IBM PC compatible and to present it to the potential customer at either an attractive price or as an attractive package; a potential target that some market pundits have referred to as '10 per cent better and 10 per cent cheaper'. The real problem for each competitor has been to make PC compatibles in large enough numbers and with sufficient back-up to convince the business and industrial market sectors that the company in question represents a solid and reliable organization able to survive in the market-place well into the future.

The IBM PC family and its nearest rivals

Following the initial launch of the standard PC (pictured in figure 1.1) in 1983, IBM has introduced to the PC family three further machines to meet the specific needs of certain market sectors.

The first of these additional models was the PC portable with a built-in 9 inch screen. Although, in practical terms, at 28 lbs weight, strictly speaking a 'transportable' (as can be seen in figure 1.2) the PC portable was launched to meet the needs of the market sector that required relatively frequent transportation of the source microcomputer – the market so successfully exploited originally by the 8-bit

Figure 1.1   The standard IBM PC (Personal Computer) with dual floppy disk drives.
Illustrated by courtesy of IBM (United Kingdom) Ltd.

CP/M machine – the Osborne 1. The IBM PC portable has now been discontinued purely as a result of competition from 'better' products from other manufacturers.

The second addition to IBM PC family was the PC XT which incorporated a hard-disk and thus enlarged external disk storage from a mere 2×360 kbytes for the twin floppy PC and PC portable to a relatively massive 10 mbytes. This machine (pictured in figure 1.3) is, apart from the addition of a hard-disk, a very similar hardware package to the standard PC and the PC portable. All three machines use an Intel 8088, a 16-bit microprocessor chip operating at a speed of 4.77 MHz*, and all operate with IBM's proprietary version of Microscoft's MS–DOS, namely PC–DOS.

The third addition to the IBM PC family is the PC AT (Advanced Technology) which is essentially a different

* 1 Megahertz = 10^6 cycles per second.

Figure 1.2 The IBM PC portable microcomputer (now discontinued).

Illustrated by courtesy of IBM (United Kingdom) Ltd.

machine offering faster operating speeds, much improved keyboard and more storage. Viewed as a 'second generation' PC, the PC AT uses the powerful Intel 80286 processor and offers limited multi-user facilities. The role that this machine (shown in figure 1.4) will fill in the microcomputing spectrum is at the time of writing not absolutely clear but speculation has it that the typical AT user will be a 'power user', that is, someone using large spreadsheet and number crunching software and requiring the increased memory and speed of this machine, which operates three times faster than the standard PCs. It is expected that the market for this machine will not be the casual microcomputer business user, but data-processing managers replacing antiquated minis or requiring a gateway to the company mainframe machine.

Since at the time of writing it is mainly the IBM PC

Figure 1.3　The IBM XT microcomputer with 10 mbyte hard-disk.
Illustrated by courtesy of IBM (United Kingdom) Ltd.

family that dominates the market, rather than the AT series, the rival compatibles to the standard PC, the PC portable and PC XT, will be covered here.

The IBM compatibles, clones and look-alikes

Apart from specialist manufacturers who aim for a particular sector of the computer market and the Apple Corporation whose very successful Macintosh computer uses its unique mouse/icon oriented operating system, the majority of microcomputer manufacturers do produce at

Figure 1.4   The IBM AT (Advanced Technology) micro-computer.
Illustrated by courtesy of IBM (United Kingdom) Ltd.

least one machine which, to varying degrees, can be considered compatible with the IBM PC family. Exactly what the term compatibility means in this context is never quite clear since even among the same application packages some may, and others may not, operate when transferred from an IBM PC to a compatible machine.

Let us examine briefly some of the technical aspects of microcomputers which might affect compatibility:

Disk drives. This is one area where compatibility is absolutely clear; any machine claiming to be IBM compatible must be capable of writing and reading files to and from IBM PC formatted floppy disks. Thus machines such as the very successful Apricot range manufactured by ACT, and some of the increasingly popular 'lap top' machines which use LCD (liquid crystal display) screens and at about 12 lbs weight, are truly portable, cannot be regarded as truly compatible. They use the MS–DOS operating system and offer a range of application programs more or less identical to an IBM PC but these machines currently use floppy disks of a different size, usually a 3.5 inch microfloppy. There are, however, separate floppy disk-drive subsystems now available which allow 5.25 inch IBM formatted disks to be written to and read from by machines such as the Apricot. It is rumoured that IBM will also move to 3.5 inch floppy disk technology in the near future so it would seem inevitable that a general move from 5.25 to 3.5 will occur.

For dual floppy disk drive machines there is little scope for improvement over the IBM PC's disk drives, but for those hard-disk machines which compete with the IBM XT and AT, rival manufacturers can offer larger capacity disks and also tape back-up facilities as standard.

Keyboard. The ergonomics of the standard IBM PC keyboard have never been particularly highly praised and it is here that many of the manufacturers of compatibles have seen the potential for offering an improved product. Some specialist manufacturers of keyboards have successfully offered their product to be used with IBM PCs as an alternative to the standard keyboard, while some of the features which have been offered as an improvement to the standard IBM PC keyboard include:

light indicators for lockable keys such as CAPS,

provision for more than the standard ten function keys,

improved key *feel* – although the standard version is reckoned to be pretty good in this respect,

improved layout, particularly the positioning of the most used ENTER/RETURN key.

Video display. The ability to display colour and graphics on the standard IBM PC is, as with most other things, an extra item which is not included in the normal price. By including this facility as standard, manufacturers of compatibles can often offer a price and quality advantage, particularly as it is generally reckoned that the IBM colour monitor is poor compared with third-party offerings.

Printer interface. The IBM PC standard printer interface comes in the form of an extra plug-in board which combines a parallel printer port with the monochrome display adaptor. Quite what a user would do without these as standard is not clear, but the provision of both parallel and serial printer ports on a single board within a standard price is an area which most third-party manufacturers have identified as providing a clear advantage over the standard IBM PC.

Processor chip and clock rate. The IBM PC uses an Intel 8088 16-bit microprocessor chip running at a clock rate of 4.77 MHz. Whilst processing at 16-bits, the 8088 relies on an 8-bit pathway to read and write data to its memory, and so compatibles such as the Advance 86b, Compac Deskpro, ITT Extra and Olivetti M24 and M21, which offer the 8086 chip which uses a true 16-bit pathway and thus reads and writes to memory more quickly, are able to improve overall processing speeds. An alternative method of improving processing speeds is to use a faster clock rate and this facility is offered by Olivetti at 8 MHz and by Compac and Sperry who offer both the standard 4.77 MHz and the option to switch to 8 MHz and 7.17 MHz respectively – this switchable option being offered because some packages cannot operate at the higher speed for technical reasons. It should be pointed out, however, that whilst faster processing speeds may appear to be an important asset, the overall limiting factor for many business applications is often the speed of writing and reading to and from disk.

Internal memory. For 16-bit micros the provision of 128 kbytes of memory is an uncomfortable minimum, 256 kbytes enough to run the majority of packages. 512 kbytes necessary for most integrated business packages and 640 kbytes the maximum that PC/MS–DOS can cope with. In this area IBM compatibles can generally offer more memory as standard at an effectively lower price.

Expansion slots. The standard IBM PC only offers three expansion slots (i.e., room for adding plug-in expansion boards) after standard boards for controlling a printer, monitor and two disk drives have been included, and the PC XT offers five additional expansion slots. Whilst IBM does offer a range of expansion boards for different functions and also additional memory, rivals are often able either to provide more functions on a single board, thereby saving on expansion slots, or simply to provide more expansion slots.

Software. It is not IBM policy to include free or 'bundled' software with PCs – so this is an area where competitors can offer packages which include some of the basic facilities most users are likely to need such as word processing, spreadsheets, etc. Assuming the potential purchaser intended to purchase these packages (or their equivalent) the fact that they are provided free represents a cost saving and will also guarantee that the package is set up for the particular microcomputer configuration with which it is being offered.

Thus it would not seem technically difficult to produce an IBM compatible with an improved specification, lower price or with 'bundled' software. Of the original group of smaller companies attempting to exploit the IBM compatible market, however, only Compac remains as a significant influence. Compac anticipated the need for a portable version of the IBM PC well before IBM managed to get its PC portable on the market (now discontinued) and from its original success with its first machine – which was generally very well regarded – Compac has now extended its range of machines to include rivals to the PC XT and PC AT.

To fill the gap left by

(a) the many small companies that could not stand the

pace in terms of generating the volume of sales required to convince the market that there was a longer-term future in buying from that source and/or

(b) the overall expansion of the microcomputer market generally

one has witnessed the arrival on the microcomputer scene of large multinational companies such as Zenith, Sperry, Olivetti, ITT and Ericsson each of which now features a PC compatible amongst its computer hardware offerings. To this list one should also add Commodore, whose original success, particularly in the UK, was built around the Pet series of 8-bit microcomputers.

Within the UK microcomputer market the two most successful IBM compatibles in terms of sales are undoubtedly those from Compac and Olivetti.

The Compac portable microcomputer (shown in figure 1.5 together with its hard-disk cousin the Compac

Figure 1.5   The Compac portable (right) together with the hard-disk Compac Plus.
Illustrated by courtesy of Compac Ltd.

Plus) was always regarded as a better machine than the now defunct IBM portable in terms of ergonomics, price and specification and is the machine on which the fortunes of the Compac company were originally based.

The Olivetti M21 and M24 microcomputers (the M24 PC is illustrated in figure 1.6) are generally reckoned to have a better screen than the standard PC, a smaller footprint (i.e., each one takes up less space on a desk), a better keyboard and to operate at a higher processor speed. Thus both machines compete directly with the standard IBM PC.

Romtec, a market research company which publishes monthly and quarterly reports, produces the figures illustrated in the pie-chart shown as figure 1.7 which indicates that the most significant contributors to the 85,000 business microcomputer sales through dealers (80 per cent of the market – the remaining 20 per cent being sold through manufacturers' own sales forces) for the first half of 1985 were:

IBM	36%
Olivetti	8%
Compac	4%
Apricot	19%
Apple	9%
Commodore	3%
Others	21%

With IBM and the compatibles Olivetti and Compac making up a directly identifiable 48 per cent of the dealer market (to which must be added a significant proportion of the 21 per cent 'Others' representing compatibles such as Ericsson, Sperry, etc., together with a major portion of machines not sold through dealers) it is more than evident that IBM PCs and compatibles currently make up something in the order of 60–70 per cent of the overall business microcomputer market.

A more extensive and detailed source of technical information on IBM PC compatibles to which readers might wish to refer has been produced by *Which Computer?* and this is shown as table 1.1.

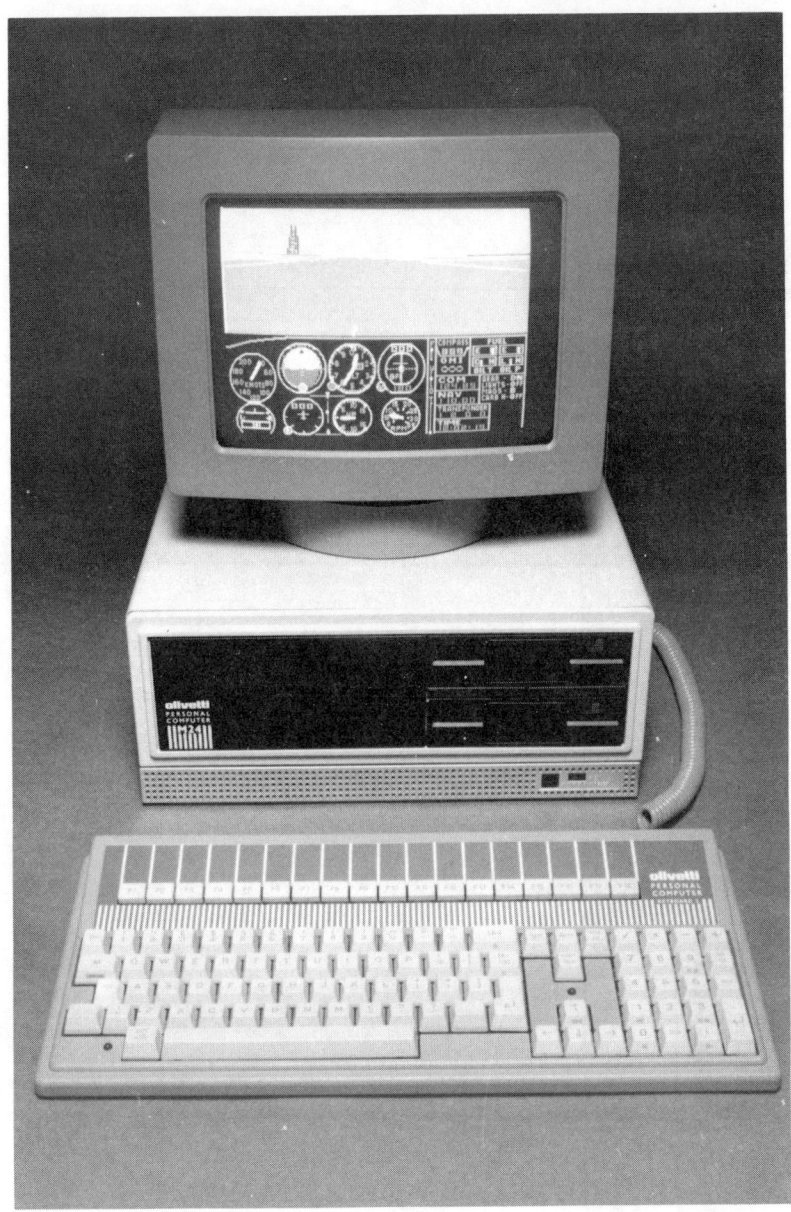

Figure 1.6   The Olivetti M24 PC.
Illustrated by courtesy of British Olivetti Ltd.

Table 1.1 Specifications of the leading IBM PC compatible microcomputers

Product	Type D(esktop) L(uggable) P(ortable)	Distributor	Processor	Processor Speed (MHz)	Standard RAM	Serial Ports	Parallel Ports	Expansion Slots	Graphics included in price?	PC DOS 2.10	IBM Memory Boards	Price (ex VAT)	Comments
Advance	D	Ferranti & WH Smith 01-353-0277	8086	4.77	128	1	1	5	Y	Y	Y	1,086 + Monitor	Ugly and bulky but highly compatible. Flimsy keyboard. Good value.
Chameleon	L	Ferrari Software (0784) 38811	8088	4.77	256 (max)	1	1		Y	Y	N	1,995	No room for expansion. Expensive for what it is.
Columbia MPC	D	Icarus 01-267 0177	8088	4.77	512	1	1	7	Y	Y	Y	3,150	Large memory and plenty of room for expansion.
Commodore PC	D	Commodore (0536) 205252	8088	4.77	256	1	1	4	Y	Y	Y	1,675	New arrival on the market. Competitively priced and well made.
Compaq	L	Compaq 01-439 8985	8088	4.77	256	1	1	5	Y	Y	Y	2,150	Sets standards for compatibility and robustness. Heavy to carry.
Compaq Deskpro	D	Compaq 01-439 8985	8086	8 and 4.77 (switch)	256	1	1	5	Y	Y	Y	2,595	Attractive, well-engineered, well-planned product. Integral tape back-up is an optional extra. Fast.
Direct IPC	D	Direct Technology (0925) 814072	8088	4.77	128	2	1	5	N	Y	Y		Manufacturer virtually unknown in UK.
ITT Xtra	D	STC Business Systems 01-236 9047	8086	5	256	1	1	5	Y	Y	Y	2,320	Competently engineered clone from a large multinational.
Ericsson PC	D	Ericsson (0634) 401721	8088	4.77	128	1	1	5	Y	Y	Y	2,129	Beautifully made, attractive looking machine. Tiny footprint and lovely screen.

Sperry PC	D	Sperry 01-965 0511	8088-2	4.77 & 7.17 (switch)	128	1	1	5	Y	Y	Y	2,195	Well-engineered clone from large mainframe company. Links to their mainframes.
Olivetti M24	D	British Olivetti 01-785 6666	8086	8	256	1	1	7	Y	Y	Y (with £100 bus convertor)	1,900	Fast processor, neat footprint, excellent screen, nice keyboard. But needs £100 bus convertor to take IBM expansion cards.
Olivetti M21	L	British Olivetti 01-785 6666	8086	8	256	1	1	3	Y	Y	N	1,600	As M24. Nice compact luggable. Good discounts available.
AM Stearns PC	D	AM International (0422) 42251	8086	8	128	2	1	4	Y	Y	Y	2,395	Manufacturer virtually unknown in UK.
Tava PC	D	Compushack 01-925 0480	8088	4.77	256		1	5	Y	Y	Y	1,950	Highly compatible, unpretentious.
Televideo Tele PC	D	Computeraid (0743) 794664	8088	5	256	1	1	1	Y	Y	Y (one!)	2,295	Not much room for expansion. Seems expensive for what you get.
Zenith Z-150	D	Zenith Data Systems (0494) 448781	8088	4.77	320	2	1	4	Y	Y	Some	2,150	Rugged, well-engineered, well supported product. Highly compatible. Large RAM standard.
Zenith Z-160	L	Zenith Data Systems (0494) 448781	8088	4.77	320	2	1	4	Y	Y	Some		As Z-150. Nicer screen than the Compaq's, but machine is much uglier. Disc drives in hinged panel look vulnerable.

Reproduced by kind permission of Which Computer?

VENDOR MARKET SHARE - JAN TO JUN 1985
BUSINESS MICROS SOLD THROUGH DEALERS

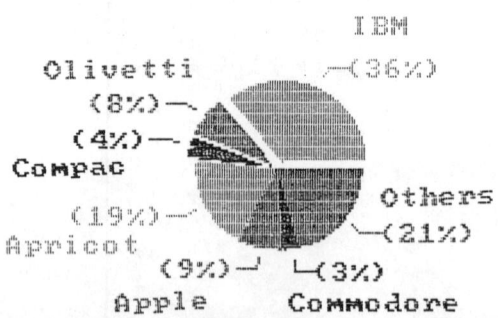

UK MARKET TOTAL FOR HALF-YEAR : 85,000

Figure 1.7   Business microcomputer sales – January to June 1985.

Published by kind permission of Romtec Dealer Panel Information Service.

Conclusion

It is evident that the arrival of IBM in the microcomputer market-place created a long-awaited standard to which manufacturers of other competing microcomputer products have had to conform. Whilst relatively cheap compared with many other capital items, a personal microcomputer, whether from the IBM stable or from one of its competitors, is fast becoming an essential part of the business and management infrastructure of many companies and organizations. Thus the efficient use of personal microcomputers is becoming vitally important and it is to promote that aim that the remainder of this book is dedicated.

2

The operating systems
PC–DOS/MS–DOS

Operating systems

To the business user or manager who essentially wants to use application packages on his or her micro, knowledge of the operating system must surely be limited to the bare essentials. Initially, it is most convenient to use the operating system to arrange that all application program disks should, wherever possible, load and run automatically without manual intervention. But other activities will inevitably occur which will require knowledge of the operating system, such as:

creating back-up (security) copies of entire working data disks,

erasing specified files from a working disk to allow more space for subsequent file storage,

renaming back-up files so that they can be re-used as working files, etc., etc.

An operating system is a series of programs which controls the operation of a computer. The main system files of an operating system must be resident in (i.e., loaded into) the microcomputer's internal memory prior to the introduction of an application package which is – in turn – a series of programs developed for a particular application.

The majority of operating systems are now disk based, that is, the programs that make up the operating system are initially held on disk. With a disk based operating system the only program which is held permanently in the computer is one which loads the operating system's main system files into memory from disk on start up. If these system files are not available from disk or cannot be loaded into memory, the computer cannot operate.

The IBM PC uses an operating system called PC–DOS (Personal Computer Disk Operating System) which is a proprietary version of MS–DOS which is the standard operating system for IBM compatibles – both being produced by the software company Microsoft. In practice MS–DOS and PC–DOS are virtually the same, so for convenience, both systems will be referred to simply as DOS for the remainder of this book.

Basic microcomputer configuration

Since the majority of the IBM PC family or compatibles used in business or management applications uses both an 83-key keyboard (i.e., includes a numeric pad) and is fitted with twin floppy disk drives, it will be assumed throughout this chapter that it is this basic hardware configuration that is being referred to.

It will also be assumed that the disk containing either:

just DOS system files (the so-called National DOS disk), or

an application package disk (containing a combination of the DOS system files and application packages program files)

is always located in the A: drive (the uppermost of the two disk drives for the IBM PC) and that disks:

to be formatted,

copied to, or

to receive and store data

will always be located in the B: drive (the lowermost of the disk drives), thus:

A: DRIVE → NATIONAL DOS DISK OR APPLICATION PACKAGE

B: DRIVE → DISK TO BE FORMATTED OR COPIED, DATA DISK

DOS

DOS literature

When purchased as a package, DOS comes complete with the following information:

a relatively slim *DOS User's Guide*,

a more voluminous *DOS Reference*.

Available as an additional extra is:

the *DOS Technical Reference* – a complete reference which is mainly for programmers.

This chapter attempts to distil from this vast amount of literature the basic essentials that a business user or manager requires to operate one of the IBM PC family or compatible microcomputers successfully and effectively, whether it be for personal use or for use by relatively unskilled staff. No attempt has been made to cover all the functions that are available within DOS because practice has shown that it is not necessary to have a knowledge of the majority of these functions simply to use application packages.

DOS filenames

Within DOS, all files must have a unique name (or specification) which can consist of three elements:

1 An optional drive specifier – indicating to the computer on which disk drive the file is to be found. For a two floppy disk drive configuration the two drive specifiers are either A: or B: the : being a mandatory separator. If a drive specifier is not specified, DOS will assume that the default drive is intended, i.e., A: if the prompt is A> or B: if B>. (Note: in hard-disk machines, the hard disk is referred to as the C: drive.)

2 A filename – consisting of up to eight characters suitably chosen to describe the contents of the file. Spaces are not permitted in filenames.

3 An optional extension – with a maximum of three characters and preceded by a mandatory full stop (American: period). The extension decribes the type of file, i.e., .COM for a command file, .TXT for a text file, etc.

A suitable name for a text file storing the contents of this chapter on a disk in the B: drive would be:

    B:CHAPTER2.TXT

DOS internal commands

DOS consists essentially of three major files, although only one, the so-called command processor – COMAND.COM – appears in a disk directory. The two system files IBMBIO.COM and IBMDOS.COM are 'hidden', and therefore do not appear in the directory listing. However, these two system files must be saved so that they occupy the first few sectors of a disk and this is achieved either by:

transferring and saving these files using the command

FORMAT B: /S

(see page 41 for details), or

reserving the necessary disk sectors using the command

FORMAT B: /B

(see page 42)

for subsequent transfer of the system files using the command

SYS B:

(see page 44).

With COMMAND.COM and its two associated system files loaded correctly from disk into the computer's internal memory, the computer is able to run application programs and the following (so-called internal) DOS facilities are also available to the user:

CLS – for clearing the screen;

COPY – for copying individual files from one disk to another. COPY can also be used for setting up batch files where no word processor is available. See page 45 for instructions on how to create an AUTOEXEC.BAT file which will automatically load and run an application package;

DATE – for setting the date which will be recorded alongside any new files created. If the ENTER key is depressed in response to the DATE prompt, no date is recorded;

DIR – for displaying the disk's directory of filenames;

ERASE – for erasing files from disk;

RENAME – for renaming existing files. Particularly useful for renaming back-up files which in many packages cannot be used as working files unless renamed with an appropriate extension;

TIME – for setting the time clock of the computer, the current time being recorded when new files are created. If the ENTER key is depressed in response to the TIME prompt, no time is recorded;

TYPE – for displaying the contents of a specified file on the screen. Can also be directed to the printer (see page 38);

VOL – for displaying volume name of disk being used.

In addition to the system files and COMMAND.COM, DOS contains many other command files (i.e., all with the .COM extension) which provide specific DOS commands not available from the main DOS files and which are, therefore, referred to as external commands.

These external commands only operate if the file with the same name as the command itself is present on the disk and the most important of these are:

DISKCOPY – for producing 'carbon copies' of existing disks, usually as back-up for a working disk in case a fault develops in that working disk;

FORMAT – for formatting a disk before it can be used either to store programs or data. Is also used for transferring DOS system files or reserving disk sectors for these files:

GRAPHICS – for allowing screen dumps to the printer of graphics as opposed to text;

KEYBUK – for configuring the keyboard for use in the UK

SYS – for transferring a copy of DOS system files to an application program disk, which for copyright reasons cannot be sold with DOS;

WTDATIM – for setting both date and time in the language of the keyboard when incorporated in an AUTOEXEC.BAT file (see page 45).

DOS disks – establishing a working copy of the National DOS disk

The DOS package contains two disks stored in the back of the *DOS Reference* manual which comes in the form of a hardbacked ring-binder. These two disks are:

DOS – the disk containing the DOS system files and the more important DOS files. This is often referred to in manuals as the Master National DOS disk;

DOS – Supplemental Programs which contains files mainly of use to programmers and will, therefore, not be discussed further here.

Creating a National DOS disk

The first task (slightly tedious but necessary) to undertake before using DOS is to create a working copy of a National DOS disk configured for the characteristics of the country in which it is to be used – in this case the UK. This disk will then become the user's main working DOS disk which will be used to provide those facilities required of the operating system. As such, with a copy of the operating system on it, the National DOS disk will become what is often referred to in the instructional literature and computer prompts as a COMMAND.COM disk and can, therefore, be used to restart the computer when required.

The creation of a working National DOS disk is in fact very simple and requires only a new disk and the Master National DOS disk supplied with the DOS package.

To create the working copy of the DOS disk insert the Master National DOS disk in the A: drive (the uppermost for IBM PCs) and the new disk – which can be formatted or unformatted – in the B: drive (the lowermost) and then switch the computer on. After checking internal memory, which will take a few seconds depending on the amount of memory installed, the computer automatically loads and runs programs from the Master National DOS disk and the following procedure has then to be followed.

If the computer is already switched on and being used for some other purpose, the computer can be reset and restarted (this is known as a 'warm boot') by simultaneously pressing the three keys:

Step 1   First having ensured that the Master National DOS disk is in the A: drive and the blank (i.e., target) disk in the B: drive, Step 1, when initiated, copies all the files from the Master National DOS disk to the target disk. If the target disk is not already formatted, formatting will occur automatically before the copying of files and the screen should appear as below:

```
TO CREATE YOUR NATIONAL COPY OF
DOS, FOLLOW THESE 5 STEPS:
__  __ __ __ __ __ __ __ __ __

STEP 1.

Get a BLANK diskette to use as
the target diskette.

Leave DOS Master in drive A:
as the source diskette.

Insert source diskette in drive A:

Insert target diskette in drive B:

Strike any key when ready

Copying 9 sectors per track, 1 side(s)

Formatting while copying

Copy complete

Copy another (Y/N)?
```

Step 2   If, in response to the final request in Step 1 the user indicates that no more disks are to be copied, Step 2 verifies that the files copied to the working DOS disk compare with those on the Master disk and the screen should appear as below.

```
STEP 2.

New copy will now be compared
with DOS Master diskette:

Insert first diskette in drive A:

Insert second diskette in drive B:

Strike any key when ready

Comparing 9 sectors per track, 1 side(s)


Diskettes compare ok

Compare more diskettes (Y/N)?
```

Step 3   This stage indicates what might have gone wrong, as shown below, if all the files have not been successfully copied across and verified. Assuming that all the files have been successfully transferred, the user is invited to proceed to Step 4 with the request to 'Strike a key when ready . . .' which for convenience can be the space-bar.

```
STEP 3.

If compare found any errors, then

a. Be sure master DOS diskette
     is in drive A:,

b. Have a different blank
     diskette ready,

c. Press and hold ALT, CTRL,
     then press DEL.

Otherwise, if new disk
compared OK, then continue.


Strike a key when ready . . .
```

Step 4   Requests the user to remove the Master National DOS disk from the A: drive and to move the new National DOS disk from the B: to A: drive, as shown below, and then to strike any key to proceed to Step 5.

```
STEP 4.

Safely store the DOS Master
diskette, then be sure that the
new National copy is in drive A:

Strike a key when ready . . .
```

Step 5 Displays a choice of six national identities; by pressing 6 the working DOS disk will be configured for UK – English.

```
STEP 5.

Next you will identify a language
for your National copy of DOS.

Afterwards, WAIT for the system
to restart automatically.


Strike a key when ready . . .


        1=USA - English

        2=Franais

        3=Deutsch

        4=Italiana

        5=Espa$ol

        6=UK - English

        0=Exit ?
```

What, in practice, this response to Step 5 achieves for UK users is that the date facility on the working copy of the National DOS disk will be set as DD/MM/YY and the new AUTOEXEC.BAT file – which has been created by this procedure – will include the KEYBUK command to configure the system for a UK keyboard. This is confirmed by again striking any key as indicated over:

```
Check that the National copy of the
 DOS diskette is in drive A.

Strike any key to continue...



A>keybuk

A>wtdatim
Current date (DD-MM-YY): 01-01-1980
Enter new date
21-09-85
Current time: 00:00:32
Enter new time
13:35:00

A>VER

IBM Personal Computer DOS Version  2.10

A>
```

The process of creating a National DOS disk is now complete and the command DIR /W will reveal (as shown opposite) that 32 files have been saved. Of these files, the six command files that I have highlighted together with internal commands cover virtually all the needs of a business user or manager operating an IBM PC or compatible. The facilities which these DOS commands offer are covered in the remainder of this chapter.

Loading DOS and an application package's program files

For normal everyday use, there are essentially two methods of loading the DOS system files into the internal memory of an IBM PC or compatible, prior to loading an

```
A>DIR /W

Volume in drive A has no label
Directory of A:\

COMMAND  COM            AUTOEXEC BAT   ANSI     SYS   FORMAT   COM   CHKDSK  COM
SYS      COM            DISKCOPY COM   DISKCOMP COM   COMP     COM   EDLIN   COM
MODE     COM            FDISK    COM   BACKUP   COM   RESTORE  COM   PRINT   COM
RECOVER  COM            ASSIGN   COM   TREE     COM   GRAPHICS COM   SORT    EXE
FIND     EXE            MORE     COM   BASIC    COM   BASICA   COM   WTDATIM COM
GRAFTABL COM            KEYBFR   COM   KEYBUK   COM   KEYBGR   COM   KEYBIT  COM
KEYBSP   COM            KBPGM    COM
        32 File(s)      11776 bytes free

A>
```

application package's program files. These two methods are:

1 Standard (non-automatic) method – loading the DOS system files into memory from a working copy of a National DOS disk. This, when resident in memory, displays the familiar A> prompt after requesting date and time input, both of which can be ignored by pressing the ENTER key. The National DOS disk must then be replaced in the A: drive with a disk containing a working copy of the application package's program files.

   The application package program files can then be loaded and run by keying in as a command the name of the main file of that package (i.e., SC3 for Supercalc3, WS for Wordstar, DBASE for dBASE, etc.).

   This non-automatic method of starting up an application package's program file is generally the one used in hard-disk configurations or where the application programs occupy more than 300 kbytes and where the second, automatic, method described below cannot be used because the necessary DOS files and the application package's program files cannot both be accommodated on a single floppy disk.

2 AUTOEXEC.BAT file method – which automatically loads the DOS system files and the application package's program files without external intervention. This method of starting up depends on the fact that when DOS is loaded, the command processor automatically searches the disk directory for a batch file called AUTOEXEC.BAT. If this file is not present, the operating system simply displays the A> prompt and awaits commands as in method 1. However, if the AUTOEXEC.BAT file is present, DOS will automatically execute any commands in that file, which in the simplest of cases could be SC3 for Supercalc3, WS for Wordstar, DBASE for dBASE, etc., the effect

being that whichever of these program files is specified would be loaded and run automatically from start-up.

This AUTOEXEC.BAT method allows a working disk of the package containing both DOS files and the application package program files to be inserted into the A: drive and then to load and run automatically when the computer is switched on. The method does of course depend on there being enough room on the disk to accommodate both sets of files. The way in which an AUTOEXEC.BAT file is created for automatically loading DOS system files and an application package's program files is described on page 45.

Many application packages are provided with an appropriate AUTOEXEC.BAT file so that when the DOS system files are added to the disk using the SYS command, the package will start automatically.

DOS commands

Since many DOS commands relate to files and thus filenames, it should be pointed out at this stage that the two characters * and ? – often referred to as wildcards – fulfil the following functions when included as an element of a filename.

Wildcards

Within a filename the * (asterisk) character can be used to represent any *set* of characters in either the filename itself or the file extension. Thus, within a command the filename *.COM represents any file with a .COM extension. More generally the filename *.* represents any file with any extension, i.e., all files.

The ? (question mark) character can represent any *single*

character within a filename or its extension. Thus the filename CHAPTER?.TXT could refer to CHAPTER1.TEXT,
CHAPTER 2.TXT, etc.

Internal DOS commands

The facilities offered by the following internal DOS
commands are now explained. With DOS in operation
these commands require no access to disk, so when invoked
they operate immediately.

CLS. This command simply clears the computer's screen
and is mainly used to clear away previous computer
responses so that the user can concentrate on new
material.

COPY. This command is mainly used for copying files
from one disk to another. In the most common application
of transferring a file from a disk in drive A: to a disk in
drive B: the form of the COPY command would be:

    COPY A:CHAPTER2.TXT B:

which would copy the file CHAPTER2.TXT from the disk
mounted in the A: drive to the disk mounted in the B:
drive giving it the same name CHAPTER2.TXT. This
procedure would produce a screen display as shown
below.

```
A>COPY A:CHAPTER2.TXT B:
          1 File(s) copied

A>
```

In the unlikely occurrence that a different name for the copied version of the file were required, this new name would have to be indicated after the B:.

The COPY command can also be used as an alternative method of copying entire disks since the command

    COPY A:*.* B:

is interpreted as: copy files of any name or any extension (i.e., all files) from the A: drive to the B: drive. In fact, since this command copies files individually and saves them on sequential sectors on the new disk, this method of copying an entire disk can provide a more efficiently stored set of data than the external DISKCOPY command (see page 38) which simply provides an exact copy of the original disk within which individual files may be split up and not stored on adjacent sectors. However, whilst the DISKCOPY command will automatically format a target disk if it has not already been formatted, the target disk for the COPY command must always be formatted and, obviously, must have enough free space to accommodate the files being transferred.

The COPY command can also be used to save information from the console (i.e., keyboard) to a specified file. Thus the command

    COPY CON: B:AUTOEXEC.BAT

is interpreted as: copy the information from the console and save it on the B: drive as a file named AUTOEXEC.BAT. How this is used to create an AUTOEXEC.BAT file for automatically starting an application program disk is fully explained on page 45.

In all COPY commands, if the drive specifier is not used the default drive will be assumed.

DATE. This command allows the user to change the system date which will subsequently be recorded in the directory against any file which is saved. The European version of the date is DD/MM/YY, American MM/DD/YY

and permissible delimiters (separators) are either / or –.
This command accepts any date as long as it is valid
(i.e. for the Europeans DD is 1–31, MM is 1–12 and YY is
80–99, a leading 19 being assumed).

As with TIME, the DATE prompt can be ignored by
pressing the ENTER at which a 00/00/00 date will be
recorded.

DIR. This command when used without any qualifying
parameters takes the form

DIR B:

and displays the volume name of the disk in the specified
drive and the filenames in the directory of that disk.

In addition the following information is also displayed
when using this form of the command:

filesize in bytes,

the date the file was created (if a system date was in
operation at the time),

the time at which the file was created (if the time clock
was set at that time).

At the termination of the directory of files the number of
files and the number of bytes free for further disk storage
are also indicated as seen opposite for the directory of a
National DOS disk.

When a disk contains too many files for all the filenames
in the directory to be displayed on the screen at one time,
an abbreviated, wide directory display can be obtained by
incorporating the /W parameter in the directory command,
thus

DIR B: /W

produces a form of directory listing as has already been
shown previously for the National DOS disk on page 29.
In this widened or abbreviated form of the directory the

```
DIR

 Volume in drive A has no label
 Directory of   A:\

COMMAND   COM     17792    1-30-84    12:00p
AUTOEXEC  BAT        30    1-01-80    12:01a
ANSI      SYS      1664    1-30-84    12:00p
FORMAT    COM      6912    1-30-84    12:00p
CHKDSK    COM      6400    1-30-84    12:00p
SYS       COM      1680    1-30-84    12:00p
DISKCOPY  COM      2576    1-30-84    12:00p
DISKCOMP  COM      2188    1-30-84    12:00p
COMP      COM      2534    1-30-84    12:00p
EDLIN     COM      4608    1-30-84    12:00p
MODE      COM      3139    1-30-84    12:00p
FDISK     COM      6369    1-30-84    12:00p
BACKUP    COM      3687    1-30-84    12:00p
RESTORE   COM      4003    1-30-84    12:00p
PRINT     COM      4608    1-30-84    12:00p
RECOVER   COM      2304    1-30-84    12:00p
ASSIGN    COM       896    1-30-84    12:00p
TREE      COM      1513    1-30-84    12:00p
GRAPHICS  COM       789    1-30-84    12:00p
SORT      EXE      1408    1-30-84    12:00p
FIND      EXE      5888    1-30-84    12:00p
MORE      COM       384    1-30-84    12:00p
BASIC     COM     16256    1-30-84    12:00p
BASICA    COM     26112    1-30-84    12:00p
WTDATIM   COM      1544    1-30-84    12:00p
GRAFTABL  COM      1091    1-30-84    12:00p
KEYBFR    COM      1732    1-30-84    12:00p
KEYBUK    COM      1283    1-30-84    12:00p
KEYBGR    COM      1628    1-30-84    12:00p
KEYBIT    COM      1345    1-30-84    12:00p
KEYBSP    COM      1596    1-30-84    12:00p
KBPGM     COM      3364    1-30-84    12:00p
          32 File(s)      11776 bytes free

A>
```

size, date and time of individual files are excluded.

Where a large number of files are held a more specific version of the DIR command can be used to identify files with a common extension, as can be seen below:

```
A>DIR B:*.CAL

  Volume in drive B is SC3REL1
  Directory of  B:\

PAYROLL   CAL     3328    7-16-84
SCREENS   CAL     2176    7-16-84
TENMIN    CAL     2304    7-16-84
CUSUM     CAL     4992    1-01-80    1:33a
EWA       CAL     8576    1-01-80    2:19a
ASTON     CAL     2944    1-01-80    2:50a
BRKEVN    CAL     3584    1-01-80    5:56a
        7 File(s)         44032 bytes free

A>
```

When using the DIR command, if a disk drive is not specified, this command will assume that the default drive is inferred, i.e., A: when the screen prompt is A>.

Note – *printer echo*. It is very useful to have a permanent copy of a disk's directory and this can be achieved by arranging that any information sent to the screen is also sent to the computer's printer using an echoing function. The printer echoing function – which in effect toggles the printer on and off – is invoked by the Ctrl and PrtSc keys (i.e., the Ctrl key is held down followed by the PrtSc key). A hardcopy version of a disk's directory can therefore be produced using:

Ctrl PrtSc – toggles printer on,

DIR B: /W – produces abbreviated directory,

Ctrl PrtSc – toggles printer off.

ERASE. This command is used to erase files, usually from

the data disk which will normally be in the B: drive. Thus the command to erase or delete the file CHAPTER1.TXT from a disk in the B: drive would be

ERASE B:CHAPTER1.TXT

The ERASE command is often used in practice in conjunction with the wildcard characters discussed earlier and in particular the command

ERASE B:*.BAK

would be used to erase all the previously created back-up files – which typically have the extension .BAK – to create space for new files on the disk mounted in the B: drive.

RENAME. This command simply allows the user to rename existing files. This command is particularly useful if a working file is lost when using a package which has created a previous version of that working file as a back-up file. Such a back-up file, usually with an extension .BAK, will generally have to be renamed – say, as a text file with the extension .TXT, if a word processing package were being used – before that back-up file could be worked upon with that package. Thus the command required to rename the file CHAPTER1.BAK as CHAPTER1.TXT would be

RENAME B:CHAPTER1.BAK B:CHAPTER1.TXT

Note that the drive specifier B: has been included in both cases since this would be necessary if, as is usual, the default drive were A:

TIME. This command can be used to alter the system time and is unlikely to be used in the majority of management applications since the exact time at which a file is created is not usually important. In its complete form the time is recorded in the form

HH:MM:SS.XX

where   HH represents hours and must be in the range
0–23,

MM represents minutes and must be in the range
0–59,

SS represents seconds and must be in the range
0–59,

and   XX represents hundredths of seconds and must be
in the range 0–99.

As with DATE, the TIME prompt can be ignored by
pressing the ENTER key.

TYPE. Displays the contents of the file specified by the
command on the screen. Text files appear in a legible
format but other files may appear unreadable due to the
presence of non-alphanumeric characters. The contents of
the specified file can be printed as it is being displayed using
the printer echo function described on page 36. The TYPE
command which would take the form

TYPE B:CHAPTER1.TXT

is generally used to check on the content of a file whose
name does not readily reveal its contents.

VOL. This command simply identifies and displays the
volume name of the disk in the specified drive. In practice
disks should also always be physically identified using an
adhesive label and a felt pen which prevents any damage
to the disk.

External DOS commands

DISKCOPY (DISKCOPY.COM must be available on disk)
The DISKCOPY command produces an identical copy of

the specified disk. In the normal dual disk drive configuration where a copy of the disk mounted in the A: drive is to be made on the target disk in the B: drive, the correct command would be

DISKCOPY A: B:

which would produce the screen display shown below. Note that the user is asked to initiate the disk copying process by pressing any key – usually for convenience the space-bar.

```
A>DISKCOPY A: B:

Insert source diskette in drive A:

Insert target diskette in drive B:

Strike any key when ready

Copying 9 sectors per track, 1 side(s)

Copy complete

Copy another (Y/N)?
```

FORMAT (FORMAT.COM must be available on disk)
Before any disk can be used to store data it has to be formatted. Whilst this formatting procedure can sometimes be performed from within the application package under consideration, more often than not formatting has to be done from the operating system. By including optional parameters within the FORMAT command, it is possible, in addition to formatting a target disk, to:

give a disk a volume name using the /V parameter,

transfer DOS system files to the disk being formatted using the /S parameter, reserve space on the inner sectors of the formatted disk (for subsequent transfer of DOS system files) using the /B parameter.

Formatting a disk

To format a new disk and neither give it a volume name nor transfer DOS, with FORMAT.COM available on the disk mounted on the A: drive and the target disk in the B: drive, the command is simply

FORMAT B:

The user is then prompted to insert a blank disk or a disk which if not blank contains no information which will be required in the future into the B: drive. When this has been done, the pressing of any key starts the formatting process which normally takes two or three minutes. At the end of the formatting procedure – assuming that the disk has been formatted successfully – the user is informed of the number of bytes that can now be stored on that disk and then asked whether a further disk requires formatting. The appearance of the screen after this complete procedure should be as below:

```
A>FORMAT B:
Insert new diskette for drive B:
and strike any key when ready

Formatting...Format complete

     362496 bytes total disk space
     362496 bytes available on disk

Format another (Y/N)?N
A>
```

Formatting a disk with a volume name

To format a disk in the B: drive and also give it a volume name, the necessary command is

FORMAT B: /V

At the end of the formatting procedure, the user is asked to key in an approporiate volume name for the disk. The volume name can consist of up to 11 (eleven) characters and will subsequently be displayed whenever the directory of that disk is displayed or the VOL command is used.

Formatting a disk and transferring DOS system files

If it is the user's intention to create an application package program disk which could automatically load DOS prior to loading and running the application programs, it will first be necessary to format a disk and subsequently transfer DOS system files to that newly formatted disk. The command to format a disk mounted in the B: drive, transfer DOS system files and establish a volume name for the disk in question would be

FORMAT B: /S /V

After the formatting procedure and the insertion of a volume name, the number of bytes remaining free for storage is displayed as shown below. This is obviously

```
A>FORMAT B: /S /V
Insert new diskette for drive B:
and strike any key when ready

Formatting...Format complete
System transferred

Volume label (11 characters, ENTER for none)? DOSDISK


    362496 bytes total disk space
     40960 bytes used by system
    321536 bytes available on disk

Format another (Y/N)?N
A>
```

less than previously, due to the presence of the system files. To install DOS completely the file COMMAND.COM must be copied across and this will be the only file revealed by a DIR B: (directory command).

Formatting a disk for subsequent transfer of DOS system files

To operate the DOS system correctly files IBMBIO.COM and IBMDOS.COM must be stored on specific sectors of a disk. To reserve these sectors on a formatted disk, use the command

    FORMAT /B

This command with the /B parameter cannot be used in conjunction with the /V or /S parameters.

A caution for hard-disk machines

As with most other commands, if a drive identifier is not included in a FORMAT command the default drive is assumed. With hard-disk machines, if the default drive is C: as indicated by the prompt C>, a format command with no drive specifier will format, and thus erase all data from, the hard-disk! This, needless to say, would be a disastrous command to invoke. To avoid this problem completely, users of hard-disk machines should use the following procedure assuming that the hard-disk is designated as the C: drive and that the floppy disks to be formatted will always be located in the A: drive:

1   Rename the FORMAT.COM file on the hard-disk as DISKRUIN.COM using the command

        RENAME C:COMMAND.COM C:DISKRUIN.COM

2   Create a batch file FORMAT.BAT containing the two instructions:

        ECHO OFF
        DISKRUIN A:

(See page 45 on creating batch files using the COPY command.)

The above procedure ensures that the command FORMAT will always refer to the A: drive and that the hard-disk cannot be accidentally formatted other than with the deliberately malicious command DISKRUIN!

GRAPHICS (GRAPHICS.COM must be available on disk)
When the GRAPHICS.COM file is loaded into memory using the command

    GRAPHICS

a graphics display on the screen can be dumped to the printer using the key combination

    | SHIFT | | PRTSC |

If GRAPHICS.COM is not loaded only text display material can be dumped using the Shift-PrtSc keys.

The most useful method of using GRAPHICS.COM is to ensure that this file is included on an application program disk and is loaded automatically by including the command GRAPHICS in the AUTOEXEC.BAT file as explained on page 45. This is particularly useful when using spreadsheet packages since it is then possible to dump to the printer a graph viewed on the screen rather than use the package's own printing facility which is often much slower and does not necessarily produce a better printed graph.

KEYBUK (KEYBUK.COM must be on disk)
The KEYBUK command configures the user's keyboard for use in the UK. As with the GRAPHICS command it is best included as a command in the AUTOEXEC.BAT file.

SYS (SYS.COM must be on disk)
Manufacturers of application program disks are obviously not able to record DOS system files on their disks for

copyright reasons. However, if they require their disk to be used subsequently with DOS, the sectors on the disk which must contain the system files will have had to be reserved using the command

    FORMAT /B

as has been explained above.

The SYS command can then subsequently transfer the user's own version of the DOS system files on to a disk within which the necessary sectors have already been reserved. Thus the command

    SYS B:

will transfer from a user's National DOS disk mounted in the A: drive the two system files IBMBIO.COM and IBMDOS.COM to a disk mounted in the B: drive, given that the requisite sectors have been previously reserved to receive them. To complete DOS it will subsequently be necessary to also copy COMMAND.COM.

WTDATIM (WTDATIM.COM must be on disk)
Not strictly an external DOS command, the WTDATIM.COM file is an assembler program which when included in an AUTOEXEC.BAT file prompts for the date and time in the *native language*, that is in the language of the keyboard also specified in the AUTOEXEC.BAT file, namely KEYBUK.COM for the UK.

It is only necessary to use WTDATIM where it is important to record the date and/or time that files are created. The necessary response to the date and time prompts produced by WTDATIM used in conjunction with KEYBUK are as for DATE (see page 33 for US and European date formats) and TIME (se page 37).

Creating an AUTOEXEC.BAT file

By creating a batch file AUTOEXEC.BAT, an application program disk can be made to start automatically from DOS. If the file is present, DOS automatically carries out any commands specified in that particular file.

Such as AUTOEXEC.BAT file could therefore be used to invoke automatically the commands:

WTDATIM – to produce a DATE and TIME prompt in the language of the keyboard specified – assuming the file WTDATIM.COM is available,

KEYBUK – to configure the keyboard for use in the UK – assuming that file KEYBUK.COM is available,

GRAPHICS – to allow a graphics display to be dumped to the printer using the key combination Shift-PrtSc – assuming that the file GRAPHICS.COM is available,

SC3 – would load an application program, which for Supercalc3 requires the command SC3; for Wordstar the command would be WS, for dBASE DBASE, etc.

The AUTOEXEC.BAT file required to perform all the the commands indicated above should appear as

```
WTDATIM
KEYBUK
GRAPHICS
SC3
```

and can be recorded on a disk mounted in the B: drive without the use of a word processor using the COPY command and following the sequence

```
COPY CON: B:AUTOEXEC.BAT
WTDATIM
KEYBUK
```

GRAPHICS
SC3
^Z

where the ^Z is an end of file marker which can be obtained either by holding down the Ctrl key followed by the Z key or by pressing the function key F6. On having entered the ^Z character, the subsequent pressing of the RETURN key saves this version of AUTOEXEC.BAT on the disk mounted in the B: drive.

To check that the file has been correctly saved use the command

TYPE B:AUTOEXEC.BAT

and the complete operation should appear on the screen as shown below:

```
A>COPY CON: B:AUTOEXEC.BAT
WTDATIM
KEYBUK
GRAPHICS
SC3
^Z
            1 File(s) copied

A>TYPE B:AUTOEXEC.BAT
WTDATIM
KEYBUK
GRAPHICS
SC3

A>
```

If during the creation of an AUTOEXEC.BAT file any mistakes occur, it is much simpler, since the file is so small, to erase the incorrect version using the command

ERASE B:AUTOEXEC.BAT

and start again, rather than to correct any mistakes.

When the AUTOEXEC.BAT file has been correctly installed on the application program disk together with:

DOS system files including COMMAND.COM,

the necessary command files invoked in AUTOEXEC.BAT,

the application program files,

this disk should, when mounted in the A: drive, automatically execute WTDATIM, KEYBUK and GRAPHICS and then load and run the specified application program – in this case Suprercalc3 (SC3) when the computer is either switched on or reset by simultaneously depressing the CTRL, ALT and DEL keys.

Conclusion

This chapter has detailed the few, but necessary, commands and functions of the operating systems PC–DOS (for IBM PCs) and MS–DOS (for compatibles) that a business user or manager requires to know when predominantly using application packages. A summary of the internal and external commands described in this chapter now follow in alphabetical order.

Summary of DOS commands

CLS (Internal command – page 32) clears the screen.

COPY (Internal command – page 32) copies individual files, usually from the A: drive to the B: drive, thus

COPY A:CHAPTER2.TXT B:

DATE (Internal command – page 33) sets system date which in European format is DD/MM/YY, US format MM/DD/YY.

DIR (Internal command – page 34) produces a directory of the specified disk. The command

    DIR B:

produces a full directory, whereas

    DIR /W

produces a widened, abbreviated form of the directory.

DISKCOPY (External command – DISKCOPY.COM must be on disk – page 38) produces a 'carbon copy' of the source disk (usually in the A: drive) on the target disk (usually in the B: drive), thus

    DISKCOPY A: B:

ERASE (Internal command – page 36) erases a specified file from disk, thus

    ERASE B:CHAPTER2.TXT

would erase the file CHAPTER2.TXT from a disk mounted in the B: drive and

    ERASE B:*.BAK

would erase all files with the extension .BAK.

FORMAT (External command – FORMAT.COM must be on disk – page 39) formats the specified (or target) disk. There are several options with this command, namely

FORMAT B: /V – formats the disk in the B: drive and asks for a volume name

FORMAT B: /S – formats the disk in the B: drive and transfers DOS system files

FORMAT B: /B – formats disk in the B: drive and reserves sectors for subsequent transfer of DOS system files using the SYS command.

GRAPHICS (External command – GRAPHICS.COM must be on disk – page 43) when loaded allows a graphics display on the screen to be dumped to the printer using the key combination Shift-PrtSc.

KEYBUK (External command – KEYBUK.COM must be on disk – page 43) when loaded configures the keyboard for use in the UK.

RENAME (Internal command – page 37) used to rename files, particularly back-up files with the extension .BAK thus

    RENAME B:CHAPTER2.BAK B:CHAPTER2.TXT

SYS (External command – SYS.COM must be on disk – page 43) transfers DOS system files from National DOS disk in the A: drive to target disk in the B: drive which has been formatted with FORMAT B: /B to reserve required sectors thus

    SYS B:

TIME (Internal command – page 37) used to set system time in the form HH/MM/SS/XX.

TYPE (Internal command – page 38) used to display contents of specified file on screen thus

    TYPE B:CHAPTER2.TXT

Contents can be echoed to the printer if printer toggled on with Ctrl-PrtSc.

VOL (Internal command – page 38) displays volume name of specified disk

WTDATIM (WTDATIM.COM must be on disk – page 44) when included in an AUTOEXEC.BAT file initiates DATE and TIME prompts in language of specified keyboard.

3

Word processing packages

General concept of word processing

Word processing is the most popular of microcomputer applications. For the professional typist a word processing package offers both improved quality of output and increased productivity. For the 'two-fingered' amateur a word processing package offers a facility for achieving a printed document of professional quality within which the accuracy of spelling can also be checked. For both amateur and professional, with text stored as files on disk, existing documents can be completely reconstructed and new documents formed from sections of several existing documents. This ability to manipulate textual information can cut down enormously on the amount of time required to produce printed documents, particularly those which have features in common with previously created documents.

For the business user of a word processing package on a personal computer a feature known as 'mailmerging' allows him or her to print what appear to be personalized individual letters to all, or alternatively a selected group of, customers or clients. A similar facility can of course also be used to send general sales literature by printing all or selected customer addresses onto adhesive labels mounted on continuous stationery.

On microcomputers such as the IBM PC family and compatibles operating with 5.25 inch disks, the equivalent of about 500 A4 sized pages at approximately 2,000 characters per page can easily be held on a single disk. Where a substantial amount of printing is involved, it is possible to transfer to a printer buffer in a matter of seconds text which may take up to ten minutes to be printed. Such printer buffers can either be incorporated in the printer or purchased as a separate hardware item. This facility frees the microcomputer for further work while printing is in progress.

Word processing packages tend to cost between £250 and £450 depending on the range of facilities offered. In particular 'mailmerging' and 'spellchecking' are usually offered (if they are available for the package in question) as additional packages. Most word processing packages can accept files from spreadsheet packages for incorporation into reports, etc., but such files must have been saved originally from the spreadsheet package as text files suitable for such transfer.

Since the advent of 16-bit microcomputers with their additional storage facilities, a larger portion of which can now be reserved for supporting the screen, many word processing packages can now display text on the screen in the exact form that that text will appear when printed. This so-called 'WYSIWYG' (pronounced Wizzywig) presentation – where WYSIWYG stands for What You See Is What You Get – is able to display italics, superscript, subscript, etc., either as they would appear when printed or appearing in different colours. Older style packages from the 8-bit microcomputer era and those which have not been updated to make full use of the additional storage facilities offered by 16-bit machines generally make use of embedded control characters on the screen to identify such print characteristics.

A feature which may be required of a word processing package, particularly for business applications, is that necessary for the preparation of long documents for which it is often sensible (or sometimes necessary if there is a file size limit) to store the completed text of the document in several different files. Where this is done, it is necessary, if page numbering for the complete document is to remain consecutive, to be able to specify within each constituent file at what number page numbering should start. If such documents also require 'headers' – text which is repeated at the top of every page – it is essential to ensure that the package under consideration incorporates this facility.

Another useful facility, which is not available in all word processing packages, is the ability to save small sections of frequently used text to be stored on disk and retrieved into a new document by the pressing of a single key combination. This is a particularly useful facility in the preparation of letters where address and style of ending (i.e., yours faithfully, yours sincerely, etc., followed by the writer's title) can be held in this way. For readers who already have a word processing package which does not have this facility, it is possible to purchase a separate, general purpose package such as Prokey, Smartkey, Magic Keyboard and Keyworks costing in the region of £75, which will operate in conjunction with most other packages – including word processing – and which can be used to store a series of characters under any specified key combination for subsequent recall.

Obviously, for single page letters, it is also necessary to exclude automatic page numbering, while another useful facility which is not available in all word processing packages, but which is of particular use to authors, is a word count.

As well as using a specific word processing package, all Integrated Business Packages offer a word processing component which is linked with spreadsheet, graphics and database components. The facilities offered in the word processing component of such integrated packages are not generally as good as those in packages that only perform word processing, except where that word processing component can operate as a stand-alone word processor in its own right. (See page 123 for a discussion of disk based integrated business packages.)

Editing and presentation facilities

The following editing and presentation facilities are available on most word processing packages, the better of which display the document being typed on the micro-computer's screen as it will appear when printed together with additional information for control functions:

Corrections. The cursor's position controls where characters are placed and since the cursor can be positioned anywhere on the computer screen, corrections are effected simply by typing over the incorrect character (i.e., the cursor is said to be in an 'over-type' mode). Although the appearance of the cursor varies, in many systems it is represented by the underline character and in some configurations it flashes on and off.

Insertions and deletions. Single characters, whole words, sentences or paragraphs can be deleted using control commands. In many packages insertion is effected by putting the cursor in the 'insert' mode, after which inserted text moves existing text to the right to make room. In some packages, on insertion existing text following the position of insertion is temporarily moved to the bottom of the screen.

Search/Find and/or Replace. Where a particular word or series of characters (a name, part number, specification number, etc.) appears repeatedly in a document and requires changing, the operator can specify the word to be changed and the new word to replace it and the word will be automatically located and optionally replaced for all occurrences throughout the document. By specifying that partial words be replaced both plural and singular versions of nouns can be accommodated.

Moving. Where a section of text has to be moved from one part of a document to another, the operator can indicate the starting and finishing points of the text to be moved and the position to which it is to be moved. Such a section of text can be replicated in several different places within a document and also saved to disk as a new text file if required.

Paging. As soon as one page is full, a new page is automatically initiated, but a new page can be 'forced' at any time if this is required for clarity of presentation, context, etc.

Justification. Justification of the right-hand margin is normal on most word processing packages but can be removed if required. A letter looks more personal without right-hand justification, whereas a formal report appears much tidier with it (compare figures 3.2 and 3.4).

Centring, underlining and highlighting. Headings can be emphasized using any of these three facilities. Centring ensures that a heading will remain at the centre of the page irrespective of the page width. Headings can be highlighted by underlining or by overprinting so that the *emboldened* heading appears in more prominent characters. With some printers it is possible to achieve a *reverse* heading, that is, white on black.

Line spacing. Text is normally stored on a basis of single spacing but can subsequently be printed double or triple spaced.

Proportional spacing. On a printer with the ability to space characters proportionally, the product can look more like print than typing. Narrow characters such as 'i' take up less space than larger ones such as 'm' instead of all printed characters requiring equal (maximum) spacing.

Page width. Word processing packages allow the user to vary the page width. This facility may be necessary for different printers and/or different widths of stationery.

Instruction Manual Test Document

This document is provided with the WORDCRAFT 80 word processor and is
intended to show you how to use many of WORDCRAFT 80's features.

                    Note that this section of the
                    document is written in the
                    middle of a page. This has
                    been achieved by using the
                    RULER facility so that the left
                    and right hand margins have
                    been reset to column 20 and
                    column 50 respectively.

Page widths can be altered at any time either for the entire
document by changing the total number of columns available or by
using the RULER facility.

Note that the document is now
limited to 35 columns wide,
this was achieved by changing
the right hand margin to column
35 and leaving the left hand
margin at 5.

The table of numbers below was produced using the TAB settings of
the RULER:

500	3000	4000	8000	250
8520	8954	7854	8564	7410
	8974	8965	8520	9630
.789	8745	595	25	89521

Note here that a straightforward use of the TAB feature does not
align the decimal point; this can be done using the DECIMAL TAB
feature as shown on the next page.

78.50	2.25	56.32	89.56
2.50	89745.2564	5.0	1.2
4568.0	25.0	63	75.20
.5682	.002	32.1	

You will notice that all the decimal points have now been aligned
- this was done automatically by WORDCRAFT 80.

Besides the normal TAB facilities it is also possible to use
INDENTATION as in the example below:

            This paragraph has been set to start at
            column 10 and end at column 50 - this was
            achieved by resetting the left and right
            hand margins. We may now wish to have
            sub-paragraphs within this paragraph,
            each of which may require a heading.

            a)   This has been done by using the
                 INDENTATION feature, so that after
                 the heading letter, the rest of the
                 sub paragraph is indented from the
                 left hand margin.

            b)   Here we have a second sub-paragraph
                 complete with its own sub-heading.

            c)   These RULER facilities are extremely
                 useful in the production of
                 technical documents and manuals -
                 such as the one you are reading
                 about WORDCRAFT 80.

*Figure 3.1   Illustration of some of the facilities available
on the word processing package WORDCRAFT.*

Page offset. To accommodate the printing of text material to be copied back-to-back for inclusion in bound documentation, some packages offer a page offset facility which operates on alternate pages.

Tabbing and indentation. Tabs can be set in much the same way as on a traditional typewriter. However, an advantage of the word processing package is that the positions of tab setting can be indicated on the screen. Decimal tabs can also be set to ensure that in a column of figures the decimal place remains in the same relative position and right-handed tabs ensure right-hand justification of text entries at the position of the tab setting.

Indentation is, in effect, an automatic tabbing facility which can be turned on and off and is used to indent subparagraphs, etc. It differs from tabbing, however, in that in subsequent editing the indentation controls the whole paragraph rather than individual lines within that paragraph.

Setting headers and trailers. Particularly for document work, a header (a heading at the top of the page) and/or a trailer (a heading at the bottom of the page) can be printed on every page simply by keying in the heading at the beginning. For documents produced in book form, left-hand and right-hand headers can be printed on alternate pages.

Page numbering. For long documents which have to be saved as several text files, it is necessary to be able to specify the page number at which numbering for each file starts so that overall numbering within the document appears sequentially. For single page letters it is necessary to suppress page number printing.

Buffered keys. Because key depressions put information into the computer's store, rather than, as in the case of conventional typewriters, directly on to paper via a mechanical or electro-mechanical linkage, there is no effective speed restriction as to how fast information can be keyed into a word processing package. While there might be a delay in the keyed character appearing on the computer screen, the buffer store ensures that all characters keyed in are retained. This allows typists to operate more quickly with the assurance that any mistakes caused by the higher typing rate can easily be corrected.

Example. Many of the facililties of a typical word processing package are demonstrated in figure 3.1 which was produced by the WORDCRAFT package. Note the high quality of print produced by a daisy-wheel printer.

Control or organizational facilities

Once a document has been created and stored on disk by a word processing package, the following control or organizational facilities are usually available. It is these facilities which really differentiate a word processing package from an electronic typewriter.

Merging files. Since it is possible to extract sections of existing text files and save them to disk as small, renamed files, it is subsequently possible to create new documents by combining these smaller files. This ability to manipulate sections of text for the creation of new documents is a tremendous source of time-saving in many business and management situations since in practice it is found that many new documents are very similar in content to previously created documents.

Printing files. Once a completed document has been saved as a named file, which can normally consist of up to 20 pages of A4 text, it can be printed on a dotmatrix printer with 'correspondence' or 'near letter' quality print or on a daisy-wheel printer with 'letter' quality print.

Stationery. If continuous stationery is used, printing can also be continuous. For single sheets, the printer will pause as the end of each page for a fresh sheet of paper to be inserted. A slightly more expensive solution is to use a cut sheet feed, a hopper fed device which allows the printing of up to 500 single A4 sheets treated, in effect, as continuous stationery. The use of single sheets allows headed notepaper to be used. For repeated printing of a specific document, such as an invoice, the user can purchase pre-printed continuous stationery.

Mailmerging

As has been indicated earlier, one of the most useful organizational facilities available in a word processing package for business applications is the ability to send what appear to be personalized letters to all, or selected, customers or clients. This mailmerging facility, which is either provided as an integral element of the basic word processing package or as an optional extra to the main package, provides the following facilities.

Fill points. Where a standard letter is stored as a document it is often necessary later to insert small sections of text such as the current date individually. This is achieved by creating, in advance, 'fill' points where such information can be specifically inserted. In the specimen letter shown in figure 3.2, such fill points are shown by the characters ← and in the completed letter (figure 3.4) the two fill points have been used to enter the current date and the date of a telephone conversation.

Address points. So that the same letter can be sent to a number of different people, address points can be specified and filled automatically from a file of addresses. In figure 3.2 the positions of address points are specified by the characters ← A, ← B, ← C and ← D. These address points indicate where the address is to be typed so that it can line up with the transparent section of a window envelope.

```
←A
→B
←C
→D
═

Dear ←E

      Further  to our  telephone conversation  of ←,  I have  pleasure in
enclosing  some  brochures  describing  the micro-computer  equipment that
Brown & Plank Systems could provide.

      The details of the services we can provide can  best be  presented by
your  visiting  our  establishment  where  we  maintain  a  fully equipped
demonstration room with all the latest  hardware and  software.Should this
not be convenient, we can arrange for one of our senior representatives to
visit  you  but, as  you will  readily understand,  with the  small profit
margin involved it will be necessary for us to  make a  charge for  such a
visit. The amount of the charge will depend on distance and time taken.

      We look forward to your response.


                        Yours sincerely,




                        P. G. Brownly,
                        Sales Director.
```

Figure 3.2   Specimen letter with fill, address and greeting points. The letter was printed by an Olympia electronic typewriter using a daisy-wheel.

Greeting points. A separate character ← E allows for the insertion of the appropriate greeting, formal or informal. Such a greeting will be filled from a greeting (American: Salutation) field held as part of the addressee's record in the appropriate data base file.

Lists of addresses and greetings. To insert addresses and greetings automatically into standard letters it is first necessary to create a file of such addresses and the appropriate greetings as shown in figure 3.3. Once such a file has been created and stored, letters can be sent either to all addressees, or those specified by number or only those meeting certain criteria such as all customers in Birmingham or all customers with an annual turnover in excess of £50,000.

Mrs. Brown.
17. The Drive.
Barwell.
Leicester.
Mrs. Brown.

Mrs. D. Green.
26. Barrett Rise.
St. James Park.
Malvern.
Mrs Green.

Dr Colin D Lewis
6 Oakley Wood Drive.
Solihull. West Midlands.
B91 2PH.
Dr Lewis.

Mr. C. Smith.
106. Bridle Mead.
Kings Norton.
Birmingham.
Mr. Smith.

Figure 3.3 List of addresses and greetings held on file for automatic insertion into a letter. This is done after fill points have been inserted. The printer used is an Anadex dot-matrix printer. Compare the quality with that of the daisy-wheel used for figure 3.2.

Examples of the final version. Figure 3.4 is a completed version of the letter illustrated in figure 3.2. The letter has been dated 12th October, 1981; the date of the phone call specified as 2nd October; and then the address and greeting points have been filled, automatically in this case, from the third address in the file illustrated in figure 3.3. The completed letter, figure 3.4, has been left *unjustified* (ragged at the right-hand margin) which is claimed to give a more *personal* appearance than the fully justified presentation shown in figure 3.2.

12th October 1981

Dr Colin D Lewis
6 Oakley Wood Drive,
Solihull, West Midlands,
B91 2PH.

Dear Dr Lewis,

   Further to our telephone conversation of 2nd October, I have pleasure in enclosing some brochures describing the micro-computer equipment that Brown & Plank Systems could provide.

   The details of the services we can provide can best be presented by your visiting our establishment where we maintain a fully equipped demonstration room with all the latest hardware and software.Should this not be convenient, we can arrange for one of our senior representatives to visit you but, as you will readily understand, with the small profit margin involved it will be necessary for us to make a charge for such a visit. The amount of the charge will depend on distance and time taken.

   We look forward to your response.

                    Yours sincerely,

                    P.G. Brownly

                    P. G. Brownly,
                    Sales Director.

Figure 3.4   Completed letter with fill, address and greeting points utilized. Printed using a high quality Qume Sprint daisy-wheel printer.

Printing of labels. Where general publicity material, identical letters, etc., are to be enclosed in plain envelopes, addresses can be printed directly on to adhesive labels mounted on continuous stationery. Such labels, which can be arranged in rows of ones, twos or threes, can subsequently be transferred to the envelopes by hand.

Letters composed of standard paragraphs. Where letters can be composed of standard paragraphs, for example, after an interviewing session, where some applicants are being accepted and others rejected, a file of standard paragraphs can be created and stored and then appropriate paragraphs can be specified and collected to compose an 'individual' letter.

Spellchecking

Spellchecking (i.e., checking the spelling of words in a document (file) is usually offered as an additional facility (as is mailmerge) with many word processing packages.

A spellchecking package usually has an initial vocabulary of some eighty thousand commonly used words and occasionally a facility for adding additional words. In operation the package can correct the spellings of words it knows (i.e., those held in the vocabulary) and provide a list of those it has been unable to identify. Because such packages check every word in a document they tend to be rather slow and really are not necessary for everyday business use other than in report publishing applications.

A small warning to British users of spellchecking packages. Since many of the word processing packages available for IBM PC family and compatibles originate in the USA, the associated spellchecking packages would insist on correcting 'centre' and 'labour' to 'center' and 'labor' respectively.

Conclusion

A word processing package for a microcomputer offers word processing facilities at about two-thirds of the price of a dedicated word processor. While the commands used by such a package are slightly more difficult to learn than on a dedicated system, the facilities offered are very similar and, of course, the microcomputer retains its flexibility to operate with packages other than word processing.

Such packages are therefore often the answer where the workload does not justify the purchase of a dedicated word processor or where the use of other packages is required.

Typical business and management applications of word processing on a microcomputer are to produce:

documents,
contracts,
mailing lists,
price lists,
accounts,
standard letters to many addresses,
technical reports.

Although word processing packages currently on the market offer to IBM PC and compatibles users broadly the same facilities, some are designed specifically for office use and others are oriented more towards the professional author. Those designed more for office use tend to have a wider range of mailing facilities, whereas those aimed more at the professional author tend to allow large amounts of text to be stored.

Review of the more popular word processing packages

Easywriter II. A relatively simple package with a reasonable degree of WYSIWYG (What You See Is What You Get) and relatively easy for a novice to use. Mailmerge and spellchecking facilities are available as extras.

Peachtext. Available either as a separate word processing package or as a component in the Integrated Business Package called Decision Manager. This package is not WYSIWYG and uses embedded control characters on the screen for print formatting instructions.

Quill. This package is the word processing component of the Integrated Business Package called Xchange. Because of the method of file transfer by which Xchange integrates word processing, spreadsheet, database and graphics (see page 123 for more details) each component can operate as a stand-alone package and can be purchased as such. Quill does use a WYSIWYG presentation and displays editing commands in two alternate menu lists which can be removed from the screen to allow more room for text editing if this is required. Like the other three packages making up the Xchange suite, Quill automatically offers options to the user in response to the invoking of commands, and since more than 50 per cent of the options offered are those required and can be accepted simply by pressing the ENTER key, this facility speeds up work considerably. Quill does have a word count and also a built-in facility for storing small sections of text such as addresses, etc., which can be recalled by a single key depression.

Spellbinder. One of the earliest word processing packages produced. Spellbinder offers the contrast of being on the one hand very simple to use whilst at the same time possessing very powerful macroprogramming facilities. This apparent contradiction is explained by the fact that

Spellbinder's simple editing commands can be used as instructions within a program which can perform such tasks as reformatting a document. Those readers who have been to computer exhibitions where one's son/daughter's name is fed into a children's story with other information to produce subsequently a fully justified and correctly spaced printed 'bespoke' book – at a price – will realize that a program such as Spellbinder has to operate in the background with a macroprogram designed specifically to obtain such result. Spellbinder is not a WYSIWYG package but does include a mailmerging facility as standard. When inserting text, Spellbinder removes existing following text to the bottom of the screen where the first line of that following text remains displayed until the insertion is complete, when it is rejoined to the end of that insertion.

Trendtext/2. The most powerful of a family of word processing packages with WYSIWYG facilities. A limited number of key commands are required by a novice user and a set of adhesive stickers are offered which can be stuck to the front of normal keyboard keys for those users who wish to make use of all the facilities available in this package.

Vuwriter. This is a specialized word processing package with the ability to print multilingual characters and complex mathematical formulae. Nearly 500 characters are available as standard and include italic, Greek scientific and diacritics, plus oversize integral signs, square roots and brackets.

Word. Represents the latest state of the art in word processing packages offering multiple windows and the use of a mouse (a small hand-held pointing device). Claimed to be more user friendly than most packages, commands tend to be logically defined, i.e., U – underline, B – bold, etc. The window facility allows the user to create, merge, check and compare up to eight documents on the screen simultaneously. For multibranch companies requiring a professional image, Word's style sheets ensure that letters, forms and reports never vary in format.

Wordcraft. An expensive but powerful word processing package which is configured specifically for the machine on which it is to run; thus it allows for extensive use of function keys, etc., which obviously makes for ease of use. Because alternative character sets can be specified, this package can be used for printing special characters used in European languages. One of the few packages which alters the shape of the cursor depending on whether the package is operating in the overtype or insert mode. Mailmerge and spellchecking are available as extras. The first package to have used a method of copyright protection based on plug-in 'dongles', it once featured in a investigative television programme featuring the illegal copying and selling of microcomputer software products. Perhaps the best of the British designed word processing packages.

Wordstar. Has long been the market leader of word processing packages with various versions available for the IBM PC family and compatibles, some WYSIWYG and others offering colour. Wordstar's unique help facility offers a choice dependent on the grade of user. This operates on the basis that virtually no information other than the text being processed is displayed for the experienced user but full help menus are provided for the novice.

Because Wordstar has been a market leader for so long and has been 'bundled' (i.e. provided free) with so many microcomputer packages, many of its features have been adopted by several other packages, even though some of its controls for editing are rather obscure. Thus the Wordstar commands ˆg (Control g – for delete a character) and ˆv (Control v – for toggle insert) appear in other packages, for instance, the text editor of dBASE2.

4

Spreadsheet packages including graphics

The spreadsheet concept was introduced originally in 1978 with the development of the package VISICALC which was followed in 1980 by SUPERCALC, both of which have sold several hundreds of thousands of copies world-wide. Subsequently many other packages have been developed along broadly similar lines to exploit the original spreadsheet concept, which, more than any other, has stimulated sales of microcomputers – particularly to first-time users. So popular has the spreadsheet concept become, there are now something of the order of 200 different packages available.

Currently one is seeing increasing use of 'super' spreadsheet packages such as Lotus 1-2-3, VisiOn, Visicalc IV and Supercalc 3 which take the original simple concept further and now include:

graph drawing capabilities,

colour,

macro programming,

iteration control and forward referencing,

simple database functions.

The basic idea behind the spreadsheet concept

The basic concept behind the spreadsheet is that the user is presented with a large 'electronic' sheet marked out as a grid of a minimum of 56 alphabetically labelled columns and 250 numbered rows. The novel concept of the spreadsheet is that numbers or variables within the sheet are both identified and named by their position relative to the columns and rows respectively. Thus the numeric value entered at the intercept of column B and row 7 is automatically referred to as B7 from then on. If the variable B7 occurs either on its own or as a variable within an equation elsewhere within the spreadsheet, any change to the value of the entry in B7 will be reflected throughout all the other cells within the spreadsheet that depend on B7

Thus in the simple sheet shown as figure 4.1a, the entry in cell C7 which is a formulae A7*B7 appears as 25 simply because A7 is 5 and B7 is also 5.

If either the value of A7 or B7 is altered then the result in C7 will also alter. This effect is shown in figure 4.1b by altering the entry at B7 from 5 to 10.

Each location within a spreadsheet (i.e., the intercept of a row and a column) is usually referred to as a cell (or sometimes entry) and the contents of a cell can be:

text – normal alphanumeric text mainly used for identifying numerical data;

numbers – numerical values which when changed will affect all those cells dependent on the cell whose value has been changed. This effect is often referred to as 'if what', that is, if this value is changed what effect does it have? Numbers can be formatted to appear as integers, as percentages, to a fixed number of decimal places (i.e., two decimal places for monetary values), etc.,

formulae – within which variables are referred to by their cell name such as A4, B7, etc. Formulae can

```
   :   A   ::   B   ::   C   ::   D   ::   E   :
 1:Number    Multiplier   Product
 2:---------------------------------------------------------
 3:         1         3         3
 4:         2         2         4
 5:         3         6        18
 6:         4         4        16
 7:         5         5        25
 8:
```

Figure 4.1a Spreadsheet showing dependence of one entry (C7) on two others (A7) and (B7).

```
   :   A   ::   B   ::   C   ::   D   ::   E   :
 1:Number    Multiplier   Product
 2:---------------------------------------------------------
 3:         1         3         3
 4:         2         2         4
 5:         3         6        18
 6:         4         4        16
 7:         5        10        50
 8:
```

Figure 4.1b Spreadsheet showing effect of changing a number at entry B7 and the resultant effect on a dependent entry or cell C7.

contain all the usual four basic functions as well as logical operators, trigonometric and special functions. A formula's size will normally be limited to something like 120 characters.

Use of formulae and their replication

Formulae within a spreadsheet can be reasonably complicated with the normal four functions of + (addition), − (subtraction), * (multiply) and / (divide) to which are usually added raising to a power, natural logarithms and logarithms to base 10. The great attraction for the user of a spreadsheet package, however, is that a single formula once entered into a cell can be replicated into either a column or a row and, moreover, that a column or row of formulae can be replicated into a block or rectangle. For instance, in figures 4.1a and 4.1b the formula entered as A3*B3 at C3 was subsequently replicated into the row of cells from C4 to C7 with a single instruction.

Another point worth noting is that in this case not only has a formula been replicated into several other cells, but the new formulae have also been automatically adjusted to match the grid. Thus in the cell C4 the formula derived originally as A3*B3 has automatically become A4*B4. This effect is illustrated in figure 4.2 where those formulae underpinning the spreadsheet are shown rather than the results from the formulae such as was shown in figures 4.1a and 4.1b.

```
   :   A    ::   B    ::   C    ::   D   ::   E   :
 1 : Number   Multiplier  Product
 2 : ----------------------------------------------------------
 3 : 1          3          A3*B3
 4 : 2          2          A4*B4
 5 : 3          6          A5*B5
 6 : 4          4          A6*B6
 7 : 5          10         A7*B7
 8 :
```

Figure 4.2   Illustrating the replication of a formula in cell C3 into cells C4, C5, C6 and C7.

In the example shown in figure 4.2 it was necessary for both the variables in the formulae to be adjusted relative to the grid, i.e., A3 became A4, etc. However, in some situations it may be necessary for some variables to be adjusted relative to the grid but for others to remain fixed. Within spreadsheet packages a facility is built in to allow the user to select for each variable within a formula whether it should be adjusted or not. This feature is demonstrated in figures 4.3a and 4.3b where 'factor' in B1 is common and must therefore remain as B1 after replication and not change to B2, B3, etc.

```
    |   A   | |   B   | |   C   |
 1|  Factor= 7
 2|---------------------------------------
 3|         1         7
 4|         2        14
 5|         3        21
 6|         4        28
 7|         5        35
 8|         6        42
 9|         7        49
10|         8        56
11|         9        63
```

Figure 4.3a Demonstration of a simple spreadsheet where Factor in B1 should not be adjusted in formula B3 to B11.

```
    |   A   | |   B   | |   C   |
 1|  Factor= 7
 2|---------------------------------------
 3| 1         B1*A3
 4| 2         B1*A4
 5| 3         B1*A5
 6| 4         B1*A6
 7| 5         B1*A7
 8| 6         B1*A8
 9| 7         B1*A9
10| 8         B1*A10
11| 9         B1*A11
```

Figure 4.3b Formulae underlying figure 4.3a illustrating that Factor in B1 is not adjusted when formulae are replicated.

Built-in functions

As well as allowing equations to be constructed using the usual algebraic and trigonometric functions, most spreadsheets provide a range of built-in functions which can be incorporated into formulae and also replicated as shown above. Some of these built-in functions are listed below together with their more traditional form:

Summation:

$$\text{SUM(X1:X20)} = \sum_{J=1}^{20} X_J$$

Mean:

$$\text{AVERAGE(X1:X20)} = \overline{X} = \sum_{J=1}^{20} X_J/20$$

Net present value:

$$\text{NPV(i,X1:X20)} = \left.\sum_{J=1}^{20} X_J \middle/ (1 + i)^{\wedge}J\right.$$

The Net Present Value function in a single formula allows the variables X1 to X20 to be simultaneously discounted at an interest rate i and summed over the range 1 to 20. The effect of this at an interest rate of 10 per cent is illustrated in figure 4.4a supported by figure 4.4b which shows the underpinning formulae and illustrates that the single formula NPV(C1/100, B5:B14) in cell C19 performs the same function as the formulae in cells C5:C14 and C16.

Maximum and minimum functions are also generally available and take the form of either:

MAX(A1:A20)

```
:     A     ::      B      ::        C          :
1:INTEREST RATE PER ANNUM :   10
2:===============================================================
3:          YEAR    INVESTMENT      PRESENT VALUE
4:===============================================================
5:           1        1000                909
6:           2        1200                992
7:           3        1500               1127
8:           4        1000                683
9:           5        1300                807
10:          6        1600                903
11:          7        1700                872
12:          8        1900                886
13:          9        2000                848
14:         10        2100                810
15:===============================================================
16:TOTALS            15300               8838
17:===============================================================
18:
19:NPV(C1/100,B5:B14)...      8838
20:
```

Figure 4.4a   Demonstration of ability of the NPV function to replace separate discounting and subsequent summation.

```
:     A     ::      B      ::        C          :
1:INTEREST RATE PER ANNUM :   10
2:===============================================================
3:          YEAR    INVESTMENT      PRESENT VALUE
4:===============================================================
5: 1              1000         B5/(1+C1/100)^(A5)
6: 1+A5           1200         B6/(1+C1/100)^(A6)
7: 1+A6           1500         B7/(1+C1/100)^(A7)
8: 1+A7           1000         B8/(1+C1/100)^(A8)
9: 1+A8           1300         B9/(1+C1/100)^(A9)
10: 1+A9          1600         B10/(1+C1/100)^(A10)
11: 1+A10         1700         B11/(1+C1/100)^(A11)
12: 1+A11         1900         B12/(1+C1/100)^(A12)
13: 1+A12         2000         B13/(1+C1/100)^(A13)
14: 1+A13         2100         B14/(1+C1/100)^(A14)
15:===============================================================
16:TOTALS         SUM(B5:B14)  SUM(C5:C14)
17:===============================================================
18:
19:NPV(C1/100,B5:B14)...    NPV(C1/100,B5:B14)
20:
```

Figure   4.4b   Spreadsheet   formulae   underpinning figure 4.4a.

which selects the maximum value in the range A1 to A20 or:

    MIN(Exp1,Exp2,Exp3 etc)

which selects the expression with the minimum value where the expressions can be individual values, formulae or ranges.

An additional function specific to spreadsheets is the LOOKUP function defined as:

    LOOKUP(n,X1:X20)

which can be interpreted in columnar mode as, find the value between X1 ascending to X20 which is nearest to n and produce the value opposite this value in the adjacent column Y, i.e., if X10 then Y10. This function is most useful in identifying the position of a numerical occurrence in tables, etc., as it occurs in price-break situations. It is illustrated in the third of the examples now described to demonstrate applications of spreadsheet packages in business and management situations.

Examples of spreadsheets

Example 1   Stock portfolio

Some of the basic spreadsheet facilities already described are incorporated in the stock portfolio example shown in figure 4.5 which represents hypothetical holding of shares in beers, wines and spirits, and shows the valuation of the portfolio (using prices published by the *Financial Times*) on Thursday, 17 September, five days later on Tuesday, 22 September and three days later on Friday, 25 September 1981.

Within this example, any change of any value in either the Qty (Quantity) or Price columns automatically causes a change in the corresponding row of the Value column

```
     STOCK PORTFOLIO (BEERS,WINES & SPIRITS)          17/09/81
     -----------------------------------------------------------
              NAME             QTY         PRICE        VALUE
     -----------------------------------------------------------
       1      AllBrew         1000          72           720
       2      Bass             700         216          1512
       3      Border            50         100            50
       4      Bulmer           175         267        467.25
       5      City Lon          79          79         62.41
       6      Guinness         200          58           116
       7      Highl'd          300          87           261
       8      IrishDis        1000          50           500
       9      Morland          560         190          1064
      10      Vaux             120         140           168


     -----------------------------------------------------------
                                     TOTAL   .........  4920.66
     -----------------------------------------------------------


     STOCK PORTFOLIO (BEERS,WINES & SPIRITS)          22/09/81
     -----------------------------------------------------------
              NAME             QTY         PRICE        VALUE
     -----------------------------------------------------------
       1      AllBrew         1000         69.5           695
       2      Bass             700         212          1484
       3      Border            50          88            44
       4      Bulmer           175         265        463.75
       5      City Lon          79          75         59.25
       6      Guinness         200          58           116
       7      Highl'd          300          81           243
       8      IrishDis        1000          52           520
       9      Morland          560         190          1064
      10      Vaux             120         136         163.2


     -----------------------------------------------------------
                                     TOTAL   .........  4852.2
     -----------------------------------------------------------


     STOCK PORTFOLIO (BEERS,WINES & SPIRITS)          25/09/81
     -----------------------------------------------------------
              NAME             QTY         PRICE        VALUE
     -----------------------------------------------------------
       1      AllBrew         1000         68.5           685
       2      Bass             700         200          1400
       3      Border            50          83          41.5
       4      Bulmer           175         245        428.75
       5      City Lon          79          71         56.09
       6      Guinness         200          54           108
       7      Highl'd          300          76           228
       8      IrishDis        1000          47           470
       9      Morland          560         180          1008
      10      Vaux             120         126         151.2


     -----------------------------------------------------------
                                     TOTAL   .........  4576.54
     -----------------------------------------------------------
```

Figure 4.5　Stock portfolio example of some basic spreadsheet facilities.

which derives from the formula Qty × Price/100. Any resulting change of an element in the Value column then automatically alters the total which is the summation of the ten Values.

Observers of the Stock Market scene may recall that there was a general drop in share prices at that time since the four main clearing banks raised their interest rates from 12 per cent to 14 per cent. This caused a sudden drop in share prices overall and, hence, a drop in the value of this portfolio from £4,920.66 to £4,852.20 to £4,576.54.

Incorporated within this example are just a few of the basic facilities already described, in particular multiplication and summation.

Once the original portfolio has been stored on disk, reloading allows the user to update any price or quantity quickly, and immediately evaluate the new, current value of the portfolio.

Example 2   Cash flow analysis

Figure 4.6 illustrates a typical use of a spreadsheet from which the cash flow situation within a company can be analysed. In this hypothetical example, the management of a small company intend to ask the bank for a two-year loan and are analysing their cash flow situation to help decide what size of loan to ask for, and also to help convince the bank manager to make the loan. The table drawn up by the spreadsheet package indicates the expected income from sales over the next 12 months and also expenditure.

In the example the amount of the loan to be requested can be varied, as can the accompanying interest rate. The total repayment over a two-year period is then automatically calculated, and the resulting figure, divided by 24, automatically becomes the monthly loan repayment – the last entry in the expenditure column. The resulting cash flow, the difference between sales income and total outgoings, is then calculated automatically for each month. Yearly totals are also calculated at the right-hand

LOAN: 10000   INTEREST RATE (pa) 14   TOTAL REPAYMENT OVER TWO YEAR PERIOD   12996

PERIOD	1	2	3	4	5	6	7	8	9	10	11	12	TOTAL	PERCENT
SALES	10000	10000	10000	10000	10000	10000	10000	10000	10000	10000	10000	10000	120000	
MORTGAGE	600	600	600	600	600	600	600	600	600	600	600	600	7200	6.00
UTILITIES	140	140	80	80	40	40	85	85	50	50	100	140	1030	0.86
TELEPHONE	75	75	75	75	75	75	75	75	75	75	75	75	900	0.75
SALARIES	8000	8000	8000	8000	8000	8000	8000	8000	8000	8000	8000	8000	96000	80.00
CLOTHING	120	120	120	120	120	120	120	120	120	120	120	120	1440	1.20
RATES	80	80	80	80	80	80	80	80	80	80	80	80	960	0.80
INSURANCE	160						160						320	0.27
POSTAGE	150	150	150	150	150	150	150	150	150	150	150	150	1800	1.50
LOAN REP.	542	542	542	542	542	542	542	542	542	542	542	542	6498	5.42
CASH FLOW	134	294	254	254	394	394	189	349	384	384	334	294	3652	3.21

LOAN: 13000   INTEREST RATE (pa) 14   TOTAL REPAYMENT OVER TWO YEAR PERIOD   16894.8

PERIOD	1	2	3	4	5	6	7	8	9	10	11	12	TOTAL	PERCENT
SALES	10000	10000	10000	10000	10000	10000	10000	10000	10000	10000	10000	10000	120000	
MORTGAGE	600	600	600	600	600	600	600	600	600	600	600	600	7200	6.00
UTILITIES	140	140	80	80	40	40	85	85	50	50	100	140	1030	0.86
TELEPHONE	75	75	75	75	75	75	75	75	75	75	75	75	900	0.75
SALARIES	8000	8000	8000	8000	8000	8000	8000	8000	8000	8000	8000	8000	96000	80.00
CLOTHING	120	120	120	120	120	120	120	120	120	120	120	120	1440	1.20
RATES	80	80	80	80	80	80	80	80	80	80	80	80	960	0.80
INSURANCE	160						160						320	0.27
POSTAGE	150	150	150	150	150	150	150	150	150	150	150	150	1800	1.50
LOAN REP.	704	704	704	704	704	704	704	704	704	704	704	704	8447	7.04
CASH FLOW	-29	131	191	191	231	231	26	186	221	221	171	131	1903	1.59

LOAN: 11000   INTEREST RATE (pa) 18   TOTAL REPAYMENT OVER TWO YEAR PERIOD   15316.4

PERIOD	1	2	3	4	5	6	7	8	9	10	11	12	TOTAL	PERCENT
SALES	10000	10000	10000	10000	10000	10000	10000	10000	10000	10000	10000	10000	120000	
MORTGAGE	600	600	600	600	600	600	600	600	600	600	600	600	7200	6.00
UTILITIES	140	140	80	80	40	40	85	85	50	50	100	140	1030	0.86
TELEPHONE	75	75	75	75	75	75	75	75	75	75	75	75	900	0.75
SALARIES	8000	8000	8000	8000	8000	8000	8000	8000	8000	8000	8000	8000	96000	80.00
CLOTHING	120	120	120	120	120	120	120	120	120	120	120	120	1440	1.20
RATES	80	80	80	80	80	80	80	80	80	80	80	80	960	0.80
INSURANCE	160						160						320	0.27
POSTAGE	150	150	150	150	150	150	150	150	150	150	150	150	1800	1.50
LOAN REP.	638	638	638	638	638	638	638	638	638	638	638	638	7658	6.38
CASH FLOW	37	197	257	257	297	297	92	252	287	287	237	197	2692	2.24

Figure 4.6   Simple cash flow example.

side of the tableau and the percentage these totals represent of total income is also calculated. If either the loan or the interest rate is altered, the resulting changes are computed immediately.

It is apparent that a £10,000 loan at a 14 per cent interest rate (compounded over two years) would cause no cash flow problems, but at the same interest rate a £13,000 loan would create an overdraft situation in period 1. An £11,000 loan at a pessimistic 18 per cent interest rate causes no monthly overdraft situations and, therefore, might be an appropriate figure on which to base the management's loan request.

Another feature of this particular worksheet is that if the company's mortgage were to be increased in period 6, a new entry in that position would be replicated over the remaining periods of the year, that is, from period 7 to period 12.

Since most of the figures are large cash values these are only shown as integers, except in the percentage column where values are shown to two decimal places. However, the global use of an integer format can cause apparent arithmetical anomalies due to rounding errors (as can be seen here) and should only be used where the requirement for simple presentation overrides that of accuracy.

Example 3   Breakeven analysis

In marketing a product to ensure a profit it is always necessary to know when sales income starts to offset incurred fixed costs. This type of traditional breakeven analysis can be simply implemented within a spreadsheet as is shown in figure 4.7.

```
    :       A        ::     B      ::   C   ::    D    :
  1:Break Even Analysis for New Product    Qty. Prod.  Profit/Loss
  2:_____
  3:Product Name/Number:- Bi-metallic detector    9000    -4200.00
  4:Proposed Retail Price £          72.00         9100    -3780.00
  5:                                               9200    -3360.00
  6:Fixed Costs £           (Totals)               9300    -2940.00
  7:  Design, dvelopment         20000.00          9400    -2520.00
  8:  Cost of manuf. plant       10000.00          9500    -2100.00
  9:  Set-up costs                5000.00          9600    -1680.00
 10:  Marketing, advertising      7000.00          9700    -1260.00
 11:TOTAL Fixed Cost             42000.00          9800     -840.00
 12:                                               9900     -420.00
 13:Variable Costs £        (Per Unit)            10000        .00
 14:  Material costs              45.30           10100     420.00
 15:  Labor costs                 13.20           10200     840.00
 16:  Overhead costs               3.00           10300    1260.00
 17:  Profit margin               6.30           10400    1680.00
 18:TOTAL Variable Cost           67.80           10500    2100.00
 19:                                              10600    2520.00
 20:                                              10700    2940.00
 21:                                              10701    2944.20
 22:COST if not manufactured    27000.00          10702    2948.40
 23:                                              10703    2952.60
 24:    Start quantity:           9000            10704    2956.80
 25:    Increment quantity:        100            10705    2961.00
 26:                                              10706    2965.20
 27:===============================================================
 28:
```

Figure 4.7   A traditional breakeven analysis implemented as a spreadsheet.

In this example the profit or loss for producing a quantity of 9,000 in cell C3, say, is calculated as Qty (Price – Variable Cost) – Fixed Cost which in spreadsheet form is

    C3*(B4−B18)−B11

When this formula is replicated only the variable C3 will be automatically adjusted to C4, etc.

Within this example it is evident that with the costs as specified the breakeven quantity is 10,000 at a proposed retail price of £72.00; below that a loss would be made. If a potential customer were to require, say, 9,800 to be made, it would be necessary to increase the price (i.e., the contents of cell B4) to guarantee a profit. The response of the spreadsheet to such changes is so rapid that this type of price negotiation could be proceeding over the phone with the manufacturer manipulating figures within the spreadsheet in response to the potential customer's reactions.

Example 4   Forecasting analysis

Figure 4.8 shows a spreadsheet which incorporates the relatively complex calculations required to evaluate a forecast based on an exponentially weighted average formula together with ancillary analyses. The response of such a forecast depends wholly on the value of Alpha (the exponential smoothing constant) which in this example is set at a typical value of 0.2.

Because this particular spreadsheet is much wider than can be accommodated on the computer screen, a window facility has been used which provides the user with two smaller versions of the spreadsheet – both of which can be moved separately. This ensure that a user can arrange to see widely spaced elements of the spreadsheet simultaneously on the screen. In this particular instance it would be useful to know which value of Alpha (located in C25) produces the smallest cumulative forecasting error over the period of the forecast. This value, which occurs in period 10, is located in cell L10, and whilst normally these two cells could not be viewed simultaneously, inspection of figure 4.8 shows that they can be so viewed if the window facility is used. Note that figure 4.8 has been printed with a border (i.e. rows numbered, columns lettered) whereas this has been excluded in several of the previous examples.

	A	B	C		J	K	L
1	----------------------------------			1	-------------------------		
2	DEMAND ANAL			2	Alpha1 fixed at 0.2		
3	----------------------------------			3	-------------------------		
4			1	4	8	9	10
5				5			
6	1.Current Demand Value		55	6	49	58	68
7	2.Current Forecast		50	7	56	55	56
8	3.Error		5	8	-7	3	12
9	4.Squared Error		25	9	49	9	144
10	5.Cumulative Sq Error	0	25	10	1403	1412	1556
11				11			
12	6.Alpha*Error		1.00	12	-1.40	.60	2.40
13	7.(1-Alpha)*Past Sm Error		.00	13	2.71	1.05	1.32
14	8.Current Smoothed Error	.00	1.00	14	1.31	1.65	3.72
15				15			
16	9.Alpha*/Error/		1.00	16	1.40	.60	2.40
17	10.(1-Alpha)*Past MAD		4.00	17	6.64	6.43	5.62
18	11.Current MAD	5.00	5.00	18	8.04	7.03	8.02
19				19			
20	12.Current Std Dev		6.25	20	10.05	8.79	10.03
21				21			
22	13.Tracking Signal		.20	22	.16	.23	.46
23	14.Cumulative Error		5	23	27	30	42
24				24			
25	15.Alpha		.2	25	.2	.2	.2
26	16.Alpha*Current Demand		11.00	26	9.80	11.60	13.60
27	17.(1-Alpha)*Past Forecast		40.00	27	44.80	44.00	44.80
28	18.Next Period's Forecast	50.00	51.00	28	54.60	55.60	58.40
29	----------------------------------			29	-------------------------		
30				30			

Figure 4.8 Forecasting analysis based on an exponentially weighted average and illustrating the use of windows.

Whilst the examples discussed earlier in this chapter can be produced using the facilities available in virtually all spreadsheet packages, the more advanced facilities which will now be briefly discussed are only available in the latest 'state-of-the-art' packages.

Graphics

Spreadsheet packages with graph drawing facilities allow the user to define the ranges of data within the spreadsheet which are required to be displayed in the graph and offer the user various facilities to enhance the graphical presentation of those data which can initially be displayed on the computer's screen prior to printing. Up to ten different graphical formats can be saved within a single spreadsheet file and the additional facilities offered allow the user to choose:

graph type (i.e., line, bar, stacked bar, pie, etc.),

headings (i.e., main, sub, axis, etc.),

variable identifiers (i.e., a key).

Some of the graphical output forms available from spreadsheet packages are now illustrated.

Figure 4.9 shows a pie-chart derived from the stock portfolio example originally shown as figure 4.5. This graph shows the relative sizes of the various stockholdings in the portfolio and also allows one to be highlighted by separating it from the main structure of the pie.

Figure 4.10 is a simple bar-chart derived from the cash flow example originally shown as figure 4.6 and shows the cash flows resulting from borrowing £10,000 at 14 per cent interest over two years. In this example bars are presented vertically. Alternative forms of presentation allow for horizontal bars and 'stacked' bars (in which bars representing more than one variable are stacked on top of one another).

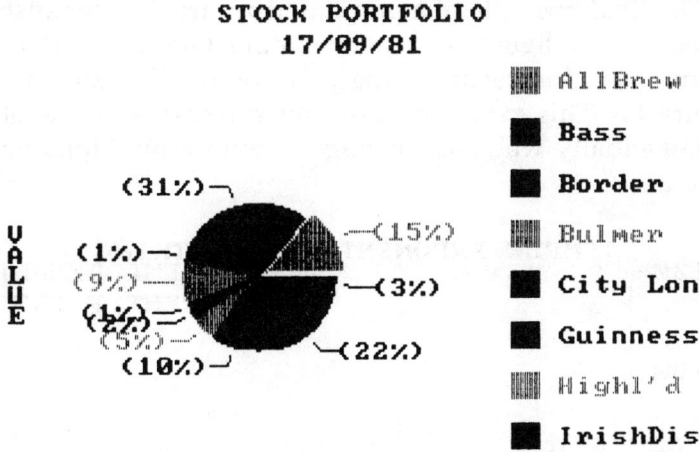

Figure 4.9 Pie-chart derived from stock portfolio example.

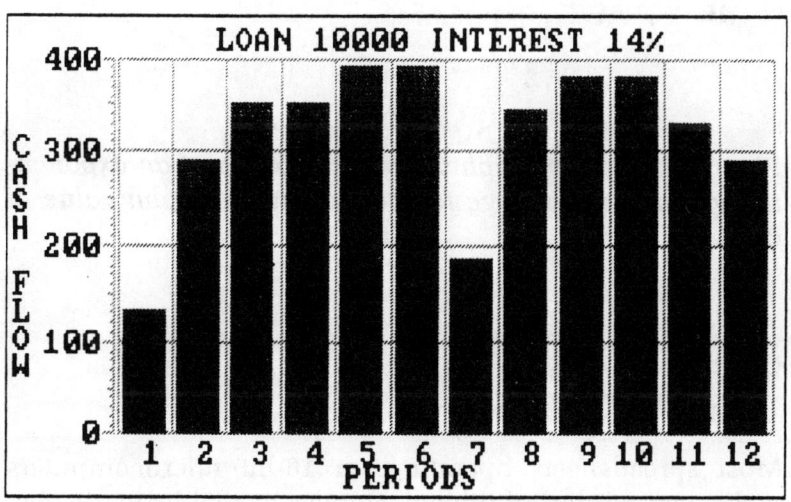

Figure 4.10 Bar-chart derived from cash flow example.

The final example of a graph derived from a spreadsheet is shown in figure. 4.11 as a simple line graph derived from the forecasting analysis originally shown as figure 4.8. This example shows the forecast response of an exponentially weighted average based on an Alpha value of 0.2.

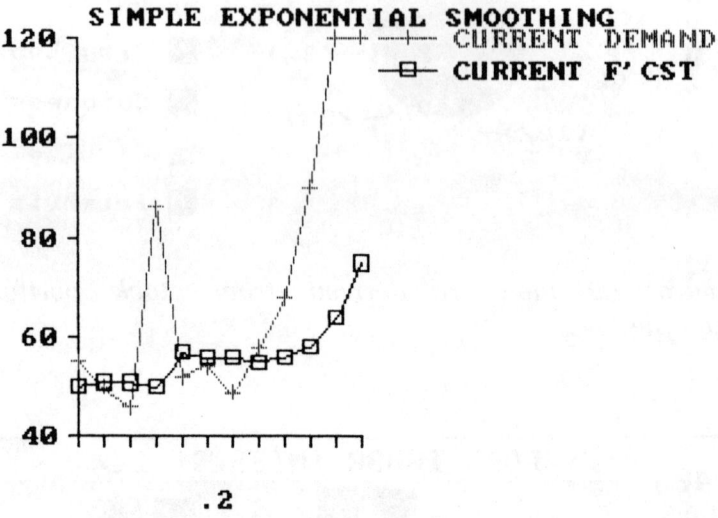

Figure 4.11   Line graph showing response of an exponentially weighted average forecast using an Alpha value of 0.2.

Colour

Most spreadsheets operating on 16-bit microcomputers make use of the additional storage available to display information within a spreadsheet in colour. Thus negative values, protected cells (i.e., cells which contain formulae, etc., which are then protected from mistaken attempts to add further information) can be made to appear in a colour different from normal text or numeric values in order to aid interpretation. Perhaps the most advantageous use of colour, however, is in the graphical displays where colour representation improves discrimination between closely plotted variables.

Macroprogramming

A macroprogramming facility within a spreadsheet allows the originator of a spreadsheet to store in a text file what, to the naive user, would be the actual key strokes that would be required to execute a prescribed set of instructions or manoeuvres. This facility allows for the development of relatively sophisticated spreadsheet work by untutored users and is particularly useful where the same analysis is used regularly.

Iteration control and forward referencing

In general, spreadsheets perform calculations either in row or column sequence. For example, in the demand analysis worksheet exhibited as figure 4.8, it is evident that calculations must be performed in column order if forecasts are to be calculated correctly. In some spreadsheets it is not possible to evaluate all calculations correctly in a single iteration of the spreadsheet, such as in situations described as 'forward referencing'. In such situations it would be necessary with the older packages to 'force' further calculations manually to obtain correct results. More recent spreadsheet packages with iteration control can automatically detect such situations and perform the necessary number of iterations to obtain valid results. A further iteration control facility is to define the size of a numeric value by specifying the size of the value stored in a specified cell at which to end iterative calculations – this facility allows the user to develop 'goal searching' analyses.

Simple database facilities

Some spreadsheets now incorporate simple database facilities based on the concept that a row within the spreadsheet is defined as a record and the cells within the row as fields. Simple search and sorting (or ordering) facilities are then offered. It would appear, however, that most users of microcomputers with database applications prefer to use a proper database package (see chapter 5) rather than the rather limited database facilities provided within a spreadsheet package.

Conclusion

Spreadsheet packages are one of the most popular microcomputer packages and it is claimed that the development of the spreadsheet concept has been largely responsible for the rapid growth of the microcomputer industry. Certainly many business and management problems can be expressed in a spreadsheet form and one foresees spreadsheets becoming an essential part of curricula for many courses in the future.

Review of the more popular spreadsheet packages

Lotus 1-2-3. The first of the packages which integrated more than one basic facility (in this case combining spreadsheet/graphics/database), Lotus 1-2-3 is perhaps the most widely sold package and is claimed to be one of the major reasons for the expansion of the 16-bit micro-computer market. A very comprehensive package (although relatively expensive) with virtually all the facilities available collectively in most other spreadsheets. More convenient when used on a hard-disk machine than in the three (1-2-3) floppy disk form – where a certain amount of disk swapping is necessary to avail oneself of all the facilities available. Lotus followed their success with 1-2-3 by introducing Symphony, a much more powerful package (see page 131 for details) which added word processing facilities to those already available in 1-2-3.

Supercalc 3. Successor to the original Supercalc 1 which was developed for the CP/M Osborne and subsequently became the standard CP/M spreadsheet package on 8-bit machines. Developed in response to the success of Lotus 1-2-3, Supercalc 3 claims to do most that is claimed by Lotus but faster and more efficiently in terms of storage. Good points for this package are that it comes on a single floppy disk, thus avoiding disk swapping, and has a simple repeat key facility for drawing lines within tables. However, replication of formulae is relatively tedious particularly if variables within a formula are to remain fixed. Graphics are generally better and more convenient to use than with the Lotus 1-2-3.

Abacus/Easel. Released originally with the Sinclair QL microcomputer, Abacus and Easel are respectively the spreadsheet and graphics packages of a suite of packages known collectively as Xchange. With these two packages, it is necessary, in order to plot a graph from a spreadsheet, to export a file to disk from Abacus and subsequently import that file into Easel (see page 132 for more details on Xchange as a fully integrated package). Whilst this procedure is more complicated than with most spreadsheet packages within which graphics is an integral function, Easel as a graphics package is superb and offers more facilities than are generally available within a spreadsheet graphics facility, such as mixing bar and line graphs within the same chart. Abacus allows the user to refer to cells by labels rather than column and row, hence Jan.Sales within a formula could be interpreted as cell C4.

A very useful facility of all the Xchange suite of programs is the provision of prompts which can either be rejected or accepted by the depression of the ENTER key. Since over 50 per cent of the prompts are generally correct and hence acceptable, this facility speeds up the construction of spreadsheets considerably.

Multiplan. One of the earlier spreadsheet packages, Multiplan operates slightly differently from most spreadsheet packages as both rows and columns are numbered in its cell referencing. Currently limited in its graphics ability, Multiplan nevertheless has a relatively large following.

Visicalc. The original spreadsheet package which lost its marketing initiative due to a long-running legal dispute with its original publishers. Now no longer available.

TK!Solver. As the name suggests, this is essentially an equation solving package rather than an orthodox spreadsheet. It offers engineers and scientists, in particular, facilities which are not available within most spreadsheet packages.

5

Flexible database packages

One of the most useful features of any computer is its ability to store large amounts of information and to retrieve specified sections of that information rapidly. Correspondingly one of management's greatest problems is, having accumulated vast amounts of information over the years, then to gain access rapidly to that information as and when required.

Not surprisingly, therefore, the majority of micro-computer application packages in the business and management area tend to be designed for database management and information retrieval applications of one sort or another, a database being defined as 'a file of data structured to allow a number of applications to access the data and update them without dictating or constraining the overall design of the content'. Such packages can either be tailored to cope with a specific but fairly common area of application or flexible, general purpose packages which allow the user to 'design' a data management and information retrieval system to suit his or her particular problem. These latter are variously termed FMS (File Management Systems) DBMS (Data Base Management Systems), etc.

While this chapter is concerned with the flexible type of package, it is still relevant to point out that many management applications of microcomputers are fixed design (bespoke) versions of database management and information retrieval packages:

purchase and sales ledger packages – designed to hold information on the financial transactions of a company with its suppliers/customers for goods and services received/supplied,

stock control packages – designed specifically to store information on stocked items and products, and to permit the normal transactions that take place such as allocations, withdrawals, receipts, etc.

payroll packages – designed to hold information on employees and to maintain and record details of remuneration, PAYE tax contributions and other monetary deductions.

Such specialized, proprietary packages have a fixed record design or format and the method by which transactions are performed with those records is correspondingly restricted. Nevertheless, the software houses designing these packages naturally design them to be suitable for as many practical applications as possible.

When such proprietary packages prove unsuitable in a particular situation or when the area of application is so unusual that the software houses have not produced a relevant package, a flexible database management and information retrieval package may well come in useful. Certainly, there are more than enough such packages on the market.

Typical applications of flexible database management and information retrieval microcomputer-based systems are:

establishing personnel files in virtually any type of company or organization with more than 50 personnel,

recording students/fees/courses, etc., in universities and colleges,

matching clients to jobs in an employment agency, potential buyers to houses at an estate agent or potential spouses to each other in a 'dating' service, keeping records of patients/treatment/drugs, etc., in hospitals or clinics and establishing appointment schedules,

monitoring mailing lists of customers/clients, directories of telephone extensions, etc.,

maintaining lists of equipment purchased indicating date of purchase, supplier, current location, etc.

Database terminology

To the layman intending to use a microcomputer for database management, it is of paramount importance that the relevant terminology first be understood.

There are essentially four levels of information in a database system.

Characters or bytes. These are essentially either alphabetic (A–Z) or numeric (0–9).

Fields. Several characters make up a data field and data fields can be of the following form:

alphanumeric – containing either alphabetic or numeric characters. Date fields which can take the form MM/DD/YY (American) or DD/MM/YY (European) are also treated as alphanumeric fields;

numeric containing only numeric characters together with the decimal point (.) or period (American). Alphabetic characters are specifically prohibited since it is possible that a numeric field will be used for arithmetic calculations. Monetary values are generally expressed as numeric to two decimal places;

key – an alphanumeric fields which is sometimes used to label (i.e., identify) each record individually.

Records. Several fields make up a *record*. A typical record can have from ten to 50 fields, which will be a mixture of alphanumeric, numeric, value and date.

Files. Many records (typically 500 up to 1,000) make up a file. Files, therefore, consist of records with a common subject.

Since several data files, each containing up to 1,000 records, can be stored on a single floppy disk, a physical analogy of a database management storage system could be represented as in figure 5.1.

Classification of database packages

Flexible database packages can be broadly categorized into three levels or classes:

Level 1   Allows the user to create a record designed to his or her requirements and to enter information into that record structure, thus creating a simple database. Records can be selected by simple or conditional criteria and records can be sorted into alphanumeric or numeric order.

Level 2   As level 1 but with the addition of a report generator – this latter being a small program created from the responses provided to a series of questions relating to the design of the report. This report form program can be saved on disk and re-used to produce the same style of report at any time in the future.

Level 3   As level 1, and usually including a report generator (level 2), but with the additional facility that commands can be saved as instructions within a high-level program (macroprogram) which can be used to design a bespoke database system. The advantage of using a specialized, high-level programming language

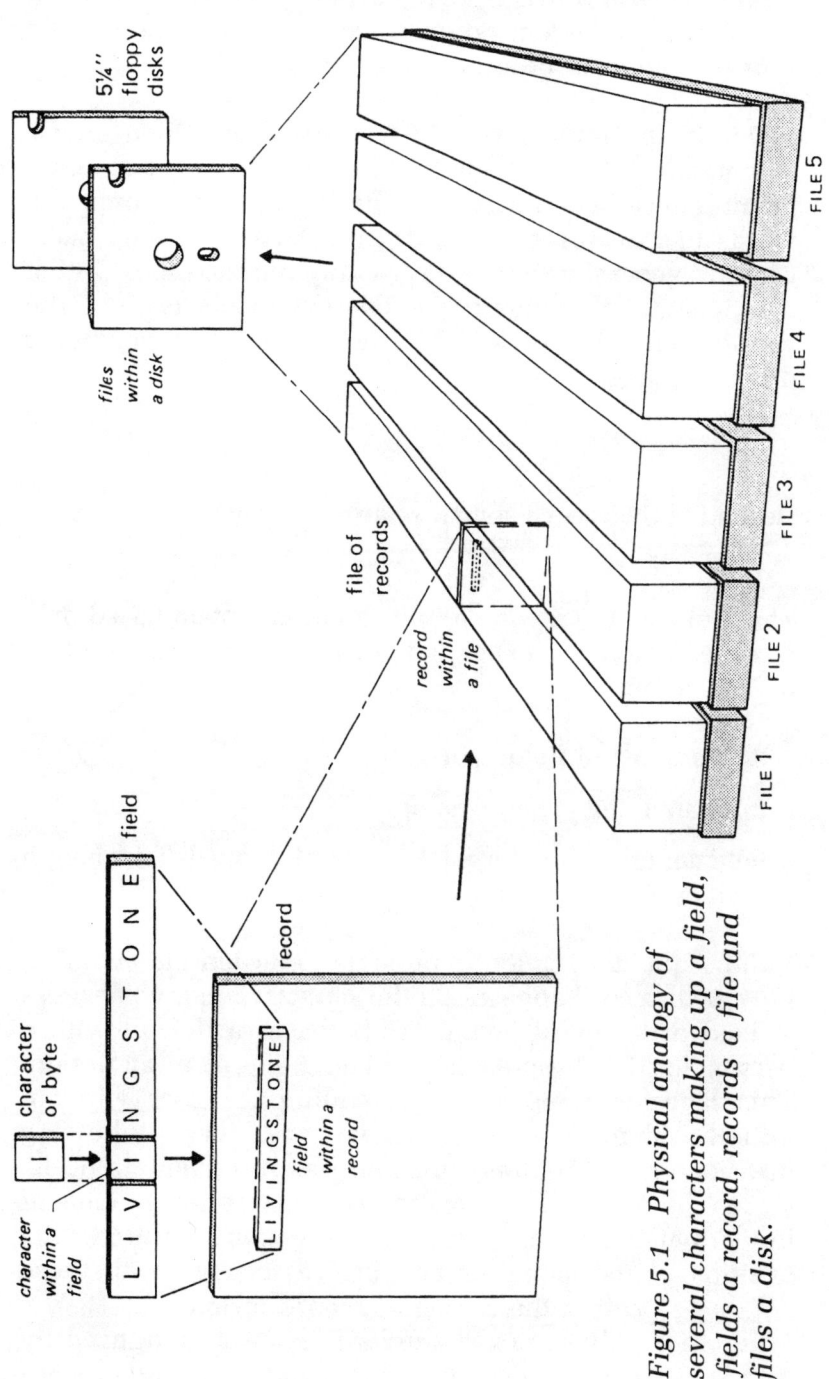

Figure 5.1 Physical analogy of several characters making up a field, fields a record, records a file and files a disk.

for database work is that development times for new systems can be cut down considerably compared with using low-level programs such as BASIC.

Within the three levels of packages mentioned above, commands can be effected either by selection through a menu (hence, menu driven) or by keying in the command words themselves (command driven). Menu driven packages are generally more user friendly but tend to be rather cumbersome to operate for the experienced user who would generally prefer the directness of a command driven package.

Designing the record structure and/or layout

The first task in creating an information system based on a flexible database package is to design the record structure by specifying:

the number of fields per record,

the name and type of fields,

field lengths — if the package is of a fixed field length structure.

Subsequently it may be possible to design the layout of how each record appears on the screen. In many packages a fixed or standard layout is offered as a default with a personalized or bespoke layout being offered as an option. This latter is achieved by providing the user with an initially blank computer screen and then, following instructions or prompts which appear at the bottom of the screen, he or she can locate the position of the contents of individual data fields and also, where required, the position of the labels or headings associated with those data fields within the screen or record format.

Figure 5.2 illustrates a standard layout as produced by dBASE2 which can be contrasted with the bespoke record formats shown in figures 5.3 and 5.4.

```
RECORD £ 00014
COMPANY      :EURO MICRO:
DIVISION     :EXPORT:
DEPT         :R & D :
NAME         :BROWN R F :
SALARY       : 14678:
```

Figure 5.2 Personnel record shown in the standard editing format style of dBASE2.

Size restrictions

Within any flexible database package, there will usually be some size restrictions such as the number of

bytes (characters) per field,

fields per record,

characters per record,

records per file,

although in practice the size limitation of a database file will be imposed generally by disk size rather than by the package.

Size of record. Having specified the size and number of fields that constitute a record (and if required completed the design of the record display) it is essential to know how many bytes (characters) have been reserved to represent a single record. For some packages a running total of the bytes used appears during the design stage.

Size of file. Because files of records are stored on disk, packages are structured around the size of a disk's *block size* of 256 bytes, and, although in general the bigger the size of record the fewer records can be held per file, this relationship is not strictly linear.

'Within record' calculations

The estate agent record shown as figure 5.3 contains 13
fields, all independent of each other, so that information
has to be specifically keyed in for each. A slightly more
complex record could contain *'within record' calculations*
whereby, for example, the entry in one field could be the
product of two other fields. Figure 5.4 is an example of a
stock record with four built-in calculations which are:

With VAT   = $1.15 \times$ Sell Price

Cost Value =   Cost Price $\times$ Stock

Sell Value =   Sell Price $\times$ Stock

Mark Up   = $100 \times$ (Sell Price/Cost Price -1)

With such a record structure entries into fields which are
calculated as functions of other fields are made automatically by the computer when information in the other fields
becomes available.

Obviously, in this example, any withdrawal of stock
would be entered as a reduction on the Stock figure and
would produce an automatic, proportional reduction in
the Cost Value and Sell Value figures.

Whilst the calculations which can be performed within a
record are not too sophisticated, the following operations
are usually available in packages where this facility is
provided:

the four standard operators: (+) add or plus, (−) subtract
or minus, (/) divide and (*) multiply,

percentage (%) calculates the percentage one field
represents of another field,

integer part, calculates the integer value of a data field,

monetary, performs rounding on a numeric field to two
decimal places.

```
05/11/81  Example of a record from the Houselist file

Address            :Greenways  -  Old Warwick Road

District           :Lapworth

Asking Price       : 86000     Date accepted :09/08/85

Reception   : 3                Bedrooms    : 4

Bathrooms   : 2                Garage spaces: 3

Detached or semi   :Det

Garden(small/medium/large):Large

Annual rates   :865

Reference No.  :S1005   Comments :Rural outlook
```

Figure 5.3 Example of a simple record design as used by an estate agent (record length 183 bytes).

```
[illegible]

[illegible]:q65657          [illegible]:me
[illegible]:Bracket
Left-hand support                        [illegible]:15

[illegible]      [illegible]

Green's Pressings Lt  021-734 5688

[illegible]:   12.00
[illegible]:   13.00   [illegible]:   14.95

[illegible]: 65

[illegible]:   780.00
[illegible]:   845.00

[illegible]:   8.33
[illegible]:08/10/85
```

Figure 5.4 Example of a record from the file Inventory featuring 'within record' calculations (record length 190 bytes).

Password access

If the data to be held on file are confidential, when the data disk is formatted to accept data records, a few packages provide a *password* facility to gain access to the file. This password, which is usually a short alphanumeric field, should not appear on the computer screen when it is keyed in. When creating a password, it is sensible to use an easily remembered set of characters since, although passwords can be changed, one still needs the original password to access this particular facility.

Sorting and indexing

In general, within the main data file, records will be held sequentially in the order they were entered into that file: in other words, the records are held unsorted.

When it is necessary to sort records, one way is simply to create a small *index file* of key fields stored in the order required. Since each record is from the package's point of view identified and accessed by its key field, this is clearly much more economic in storage terms than creating another complete data file with the records sorted. The index file occupies only a small fraction of the storage space required for the related data file. The creation of such an index file called Houseprice is shown diagrammatically in figure 5.5 and indicates that the key fields (reference numbers) of the records in the data file Houselist are held in the Houseprice index file in descending order of the price field.

Such sorted index files can be based on any field or combination of fields within a record. Where the field being used is alphanumeric, sorting is performed alphabetically. When the value of a field within a particular record is changed and that field has been used previously

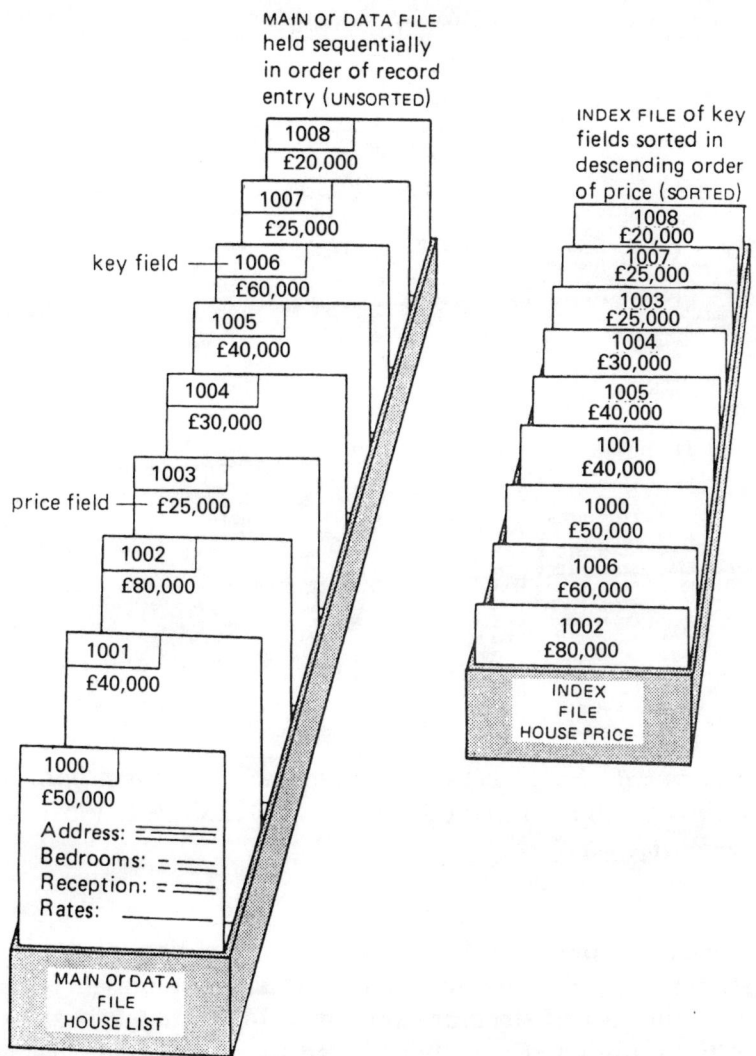

Figure 5.5 Diagrammatic representation of an unsorted data file and a sorted index file.

to create an index file, should the change of value change the sorted order a well designed package will automatically change the order of the index file. New records added to the file can be similarly accommodated.

```
FILE OF EMPLOYEES LISTED UN-INDEXED ie AS ENTERED
==================================================

RECORD  COMPANY      DIV.     DEPT.   NAME          SALARY
======  =======      ===      ====    ====          ======
00001   UK MICRO     HOME     MKTG    JONES  W      18000
00002   EURO MICRO   EXPORT   PROD    HALL  P       16500
00003   UK MICRO     EXPORT   R & D   BRYANT  P     16000
00004   EURO MICRO   HOME     PROD    YOUNG  F      12000
00005   EURO MICRO   EXPORT   MKTG    SMITH  F      17500
00006   UK MICRO     EXPORT   PROD    ABRAHAMS  G   14300
00007   UK MICRO     HOME     MKTG    BROWN  T      16570
00008   EURO MICRO   EXPORT   R & D   SQUIRES  F    17400
00009   UK MICRO     EXPORT   MKTG    LEWIS  C      18000
00010   EURO MICRO   HOME     PROD    GRANT  W      15000
00011   EURO MICRO   EXPORT   MKTG    LOESER  G     12679
00012   UK MICRO     EXPORT   PROD    DAVIS  J  A   12670
00013   EURO MICRO   HOME     R & D   BUNNAG  A     19000
00014   EURO MICRO   EXPORT   R & D   BROWN  R  F   14678


RECORDS IN FILE ARE INDEXED ON  ----> COMPANY + DIVISION + DEPARTMENT
---------------------------------------------------------------------

RECORD  COMPANY      DIV.     DEPT.   NAME          SALARY
======  =======      ===      ====    ====          ======
00005   EURO MICRO   EXPORT   MKTG    SMITH  F      17500
00011   EURO MICRO   EXPORT   MKTG    LOESER  G     12679
00002   EURO MICRO   EXPORT   PROD    HALL  P       16500
00008   EURO MICRO   EXPORT   R & D   SQUIRES  F    17400
00014   EURO MICRO   EXPORT   R & D   BROWN  R  F   14678
00004   EURO MICRO   HOME     PROD    YOUNG  F      12000
00010   EURO MICRO   HOME     PROD    GRANT  W      15000
00013   EURO MICRO   HOME     R & D   BUNNAG  A     19000
00009   UK MICRO     EXPORT   MKTG    LEWIS  C      18000
00006   UK MICRO     EXPORT   PROD    ABRAHAMS  G   14300
00012   UK MICRO     EXPORT   PROD    DAVIS  J  A   12670
00003   UK MICRO     EXPORT   R & D   BRYANT  P     16000
00001   UK MICRO     HOME     MKTG    JONES  W      18000
00007   UK MICRO     HOME     MKTG    BROWN  T      16570
-----------------------------------------------------------
```

Figure 5.6   Small personnel database file shown both un-indexed   and   indexed   by   COMPANY + DIVISION + DEPARTMENT.

An example of indexing on a combination of fields is shown in figure 5.6 where a small file of personnel records with the record structure shown as in figure 5.2 is shown initially unsorted and then linked to an index file created on a combination of three fields namely COMPANY + DIVISION + DEPARTMENT. Examination of this example indicates that the records once indexed have been initially sorted alphabetically by COMPANY, then within COMPANY alphabetically by DIVISION and finally within DIVISION alphabetically by DEPARTMENT.

The ability to sort and index is perhaps the most powerful feature of a microcomputer when compared with its manual equivalent.

Searching for specified records

After the creation of the data file, all database management and information retrieval packages allow the user to search through the data file to select records. This can be done either by 'nudging' or 'skipping' manually through sorted or unsorted files or by selecting records which meet either a single criterion or multiple criteria.

Search criteria can be set up using logical AND, NOT and OR functions together with criteria such as those shown in table 5.1.

Table 5.1 Search criteria

	Alphanumeric/key	*Numeric/value*	*Date*
Equal to, e.g.	= 'Lapworth'	= 100	= 12/11/85
Greater than, e.g.	> 'Lapworth'	> 100	> 12/11/85
Less than, e.g.	< 'Lapworth'	< 100	< 12/11/85
Greater than (after for alphanumeric) or equal to, e.g.	⩾ 'Lapworth'	⩾ 100	⩾ 12/11/85
Less than (before for alphanumeric) or equal to, e.g.	⩽ 'Lapworth'	⩽ 100	⩽ 12/11/85

The occurrence of a particular character in a particular position in a field can also be used. For example, + + + 11 can be used to identify records with a November date within a DD/MM/YY date field (since the 11 field, coincides with the MM field, uniquely identifies the month of November).

Search criteria, once created, can sometimes be named and stored as a search criteria file. This saves the user setting them on each occasion which can be an advantage if the same ones are likely to be used again and again.

Records in a data file can be searched unsorted or sorted. If a sorted search is wanted, there must already be a named index file.

When searching for certain records in a data file, the user can typically:

print all records meeting the search criterion,

view all records meeting the search criterion,

view all records meeting the search criterion and print only those selected by the user.

Figures 5.7a and 5.7b show the results of two searches conducted on the Houselist file. Figure 5.7a uses the

```
11/10/85  Houses on file since before 09/07/85

Address              :567 Warwick Road

District             :Solihull Wood

Asking Price         : 45000    Date accepted :09/06/85

Reception : 2                    Bedrooms  : 3

Bathrooms : 1                    Garage spaces: 0

Detached or semi  :Semi

Garden(small/medium/large):Small

Annual rates  :412

Reference No.  :S1008   Comments :Older terraced property
---------------------------------------------------------------
Address              :65 Bermuda Avenue

District             :Sheldon

Asking Price         : 45000    Date accepted :08/07/85

Reception : 2                    Bedrooms  : 3

Bathrooms : 1                    Garage spaces: 0

Detached or semi  :Semi

Garden(small/medium/large):Small

Annual rates  :389

Reference No.  :S1012   Comments :Suitable first time buyer
---------------------------------------------------------------
```

Figure 5.7a Example of a record search within an unsorted Houselist file for houses meeting a single criterion of date.

simple criterion of searching for any houses on file before
the date 09/07/85 – the type of criterion an estate agent
might well use to identify houses which had been on his
books for a long time. In this case a sorted index file was
not used, the unsorted data file was searched, although the
records will, of course, be shown in ascending order of
date accepted simply because the records were originally
entered and, therefore, stored in that order.

```
11/10/85  Houses above 50000 in Lapworth in price order

Address            :Greenways  -  Old Warwick Road

District           :Lapworth

Asking Price       : 86000    Date accepted :09/08/85

Reception  : 3              Bedrooms   : 4

Bathrooms  : 2              Garage spaces: 3

Detached or semi   :Det

Garden(small/medium/large):Large

Annual rates  :865

Reference No.  :S1005   Comments :Rural outlook
-----------------------------------------------------------------
Address            :Blenheim - Copsewood Road

District           :Lapworth

Asking Price       : 98000    Date accepted :09/08/85

Reception  : 3              Bedrooms   : 4

Bathrooms  : 2              Garage spaces: 3

Detached or semi   :Det

Garden(small/medium/large):Large

Annual rates  :989

Reference No.  :S1010   Comments :Gentleman's Residence
-----------------------------------------------------------------
```

*Figure 5.7b Example of a record search within the
Houselist file sorted by value for houses meeting two
specified criteria of price and location.*

Figure 5.7b is the result of a search through the same Houselist file but in this case sorted on the field Asking Price. In this case the two records that have been found meet the criterion that the Asking Price should be greater than £80,000 and that the District is (equal to) Lapworth. Such a search criterion could be used to match houses to a relatively affluent prospective purchaser! Since the sorted index file was used the houses appear in ascending order of asking price.

Report writing

So far in this chapter we have discussed the design of a record, the creation of a data file of many records and the subsequent management of those records. In addition to these *record handling* facilities, many database management and information retrieval packages also offer a *report writing* facility.

A report is designed to extract information from particular fields on either all or selected records within a data file and to present that information as a printed report. Where numerical data are extracted from records, it is also possible to perform simple *'within report' calculations* on those data in much the same way as for 'within record' calculations (see page 96). The design of the printed report has to be built up by the user and will generally be stored as a *report print control file* for subsequent use. For most reports it will be necessary to extract data from sorted records, hence a report print control file will generally be associated with a particular index file.

Designing the report

When building up the design of a printed report, most database management and information retrieval packages break the report into four elements which are:

Page controls. These specify headings, date, etc., which will appear on every page of the report and also indicate whether pages will be sequentially numbered or not.

Record controls. These specify which record data fields are to be extracted from records within the data file and give instructions as to where, on the page of the report, such fields are to be printed. If any calculations are to be performed on numeric or value fields, the print control file must include a specification of those calculations, together with instructions as to where the results of those calculations are to be printed.

Subtotal controls. Where subtotals are to be accumulated, the report print control file must specify which numeric or value fields are to be accumulated. Subtotals are usually printed and then set equal to zero when the specified index field changes. Subtotals, therefore, can only be used in reports associated with a sorted data file. Any printing requirements such as the heading SUBTOTAL must also be specified. Because the subtotal control is triggered by a change occurring in a specified field, this facility can be used most effectively to *separate sections* of a report, either by printing a separation line of, say, hyphens or even more simply by producing a line space.

Total controls. Where totals are to be accumulated for all records appearing in the printed report, the numeric or value data field to be accumulated must be specified together with any printing requirements, such as TOTAL.

Examples of reports

To illustrate these various facilities as they could appear in printed reports, several examples are reproduced in figures 5.8 to 5.10 together with comments on which facilities have been used and how.

Figure 5.8 shows a three-page report extracted from a telephone extension file. In this example the pages have been shortened to form a booklet and can accommodate only a maximum of 23 names per page. The title, column headings and date of issue are repeated on every page and pages are numbered sequentially. While there are no subtotal calculations, because the records are now sorted on the field DEPARTMENT, the subtotal control facility has been used to print a separation line of hyphens each time the DEPARTMENT field changes.

The sales commission example shown in figure 5.9 illustrates nearly all the facilities available in a report print from a database management and information retrieval package. In this example three fields are extracted from each record (namely Sales Rep, Total and NUMBER) whose format is shown in figure 5.10. The fourth figure to be printed per record (i.e., Commission) is calculated automatically as 10 per cent of the Total field. Thus the subtotals represent the commission earned by each sales representative and the total the overall commission to be paid. The report presupposes records are sorted alphabetically by sales representatives.

Although not apparent in the printed report itself, another facility that has been used is a search criterion specifying that only quotations with an acceptance date later than 05/09/85 be included. This obviously will ensure that no quotations accepted before that date, for which commission has already been paid, or quotations which have yet to be accepted are included in the report. The quotation record shown in figure 5.10 (to indicate the type of record on which the report was based) appears as the first commission due to sales reresentative FIN since the acceptance date for this quote was 20/10/81.

Figure 5.8   Example of a printed report from a telephone extension file, sorted on the field DEPARTMENT and incorporating page headings and separation lines between departments.

```
Page    1 TELEPHONE EXTENSIONS --- DEPARTMENT ORDER
10/11/85
     NAME                  DEPARTMENT           EXTENSION
========================================================
GORDON  James G      Administration             721
PRENTICE  Peter G    Administration             777
DIXON  Edward  J      Administration             707
LAWRENCE  Jane  (Mrs) Administration            747
EDWARDS  David  S     Administration             721
HALLAM  Geoffrey  H   Administration             732
GABOR  Peter          Administration             721
GIBBS  Neal  F        Administration             732
---------------------------------------------------------
GRIMLEY  Edward  J    Inspection                 606
HALL  Norman          Inspection                 632
JONES  Ann  (Mrs)     Inspection                 607
GREGORY  David        Inspection                 654
ANDREWS  Mark  E      Inspection                 654
---------------------------------------------------------
HARTLEY  Jennifer(Ms)Marketing                   490
WEBB  Kenneth  E      Marketing                  454
BURTON  Helen  (Miss) Marketing                  421
CALE  Ronald          Marketing                  444
LEWIS  Colin  D       Marketing                  421
---------------------------------------------------------
SANDERSON  Andrew  G  Production                 387
JOHNSON  Edward  K    Production                 365
      Page    2 TELEPHONE EXTENSIONS --- DEPARTMENT ORDER
      10/11/85
          NAME                DEPARTMENT           EXTENSION
========================================================
      ISLIP  John  D      Production              307
      HARRIS  David  S    Production              305
      PHIPPS  Gordon  L   Production              305
      LING  Maurice       Production              304
      ANTONY  Barry       Production              333
      MORRIS  Julian  D   Production              308
      BENNETT  David       Production              367
      JOHNSON  Anne  (Miss) Production             375
      BURCHER  Peter      Production              397
      NICHOLSON  Garth  H Production              364
      WILLIAMS  Graham  J Production              305
      ---------------------------------------------------
      LANGLEY  Edward      Production Planning     521
      MACMILLAN  Brian  L  Production Planning     532
      TAYLOR  Brian  S     Production Planning     555
      MACGREGOR  John      Production Planning     521
      WILSON  Brian  H     Production Planning     532
      ---------------------------------------------------
      LIVINGSTONE  John  D Purchasing             276
      FREER  Gill  (Miss)  Purchasing             289
      WARING  Philip  A    Purchasing             207
      SMITH  James  J      Purchasing             264
      POWELL  Graham  J    Purchasing             234
          Page    3 TELEPHONE EXTENSIONS --- DEPARTMENT ORDER
          10/11/85
              NAME                DEPARTMENT           EXTENSION
========================================================
          SKINNER  Jane  (Ms)   Purchasing          254
          HIPKISS  Jenny  (Mrs) Purchasing          231
          ---------------------------------------------------
          NANSEN  Graham  F     Sales               174
          BROWN   John  G       Sales               165
          DAVIES  Sharon  (Miss)Sales               123
          GRENVILLE  Alice  (Ms)Sales               109
          OAKLEY  Mark          Sales               109
          GRAY  Anthony  F      Sales               121
          BUCKLE  Sandra  (Mrs) Sales               109
          ---------------------------------------------------
```

```
05/11/85

SALES REP'S COMMISSION FOR LAST 2 MONTHS


SALES REP    TOTAL    INV.NO.    COMMISSION
-------------------------------------------------


DGT          895.00    2            89.50
DGT         2205.00    9           220.50
DGT         2205.00    9           220.50


               Sub Total           530.50


FIN         2611.10    5           261.11
FIN          105.00   10            10.50


               Sub Total           271.61


FNL           34.90    6             3.49
FNL          175.85    8            17.59
FNL            8.11   11              .81
FNL         2144.65    3           214.47


               Sub Total           236.36


GHS         2058.30    7           205.83
GHS          142.80    4            14.28


               Sub Total           220.11


               TOTAL              2171.48
```

Figure 5.9 Example of a printed report, sorted with commission calculated for each record, subtotalled for each representative and totalled for overall commission to be paid.

```
                    QUOTATION

NUMBER :0005                DATE :17/09/85
- - - - - - - - - - - - - - - - - - - - - - - - - - - - - -
From,                  For,
Bloggs & Co, Ltd,      CMS Ltd
Southern Avenue        20 Universe Rd
Birmingham B4 1ST      Bromley, Kent
- - - - - - - - - - - - - - - - - - - - - - - - - - - - - -
QTY       DESCRIPTION        PRICE
    1  8032 Computer         895.00      895.00
    1  8050 Dual Disc Driv   895.00      895.00
    1  Aculab 1 Interface     90.00       90.00
    1  Anadex Printer DP95   999.00      999.00
                                       - - - - - - - - - -
                          Sub Total     2879.00
                   10 %Discount          287.90
Sales Rep              Carriage          20.00
FIN
                          Total         2611.10
Date Accepted               VAT          391.66
20/10/81           INVOICE TOTAL        3002.76
- - - - - - - - - - - - - - - - - - - - - - - - - - - - - - -
```

Figure 5.10 Example of a record from a quotations file (record length 508 bytes).

Other facilities

Global or selective record transactions

Another facility available on many database management and information retrieval packages is the ability to alter numeric or value fields on all, or selected, records. Thus, for example, all *price fields* on all records could be increased (or, less likely, decreased) by 10 per cent. An example of this is shown in figure 5.11 using the package dBASE II and the keyed in instruction:

REPLACE ALL PRICE WITH PRICE*1.1

where ALL means all records and PRICE is the field to be changed.

A further sophistication offered by this package, also illustrated is *selective* transactions. The instruction:

REPLACE FOR SIZE = 'EIGHT INCH' PRICE WITH PRICE + .10

increases the price of only the 8 inch disks by a further 10p.

Macroprogramming

A few database management and information retrieval packages offer a very powerful facility known as macro-programming, which allows the user to write programs made up of many instructions, each of which would normally have to be an individually keyed in instruction. Hence the instruction:

REPLACE ALL PRICE WITH PRICE*1.1

which was keyed into the computer to produce part of figure 5.11 although *one* instruction at the macro level would, however, be automatically translated into *many* instructions in a lower level language.

This macroprogramming facility is a powerful tool which can be used to design bespoke database applications much more rapidly than by using a normal, lower level language such as BASIC. The advantage is illustrated in the following example using the dBASE II macro-programming facility.

Consider the following four-instruction program:

```
USE DFILE INDEX DFIND
ERASE
REPLACE ALL PRICE WITH PRICE*1.1
DISPLAY ALL FOR PRICE > 10.00 .AND. PRICE < 100
```

This simple little program instructs the computer to use a database file (DFILE) whose records are sorted in alpha-

```
                    PRICE LIST FOR FIVE AND EIGHT INCH FLOPPY DISKS

        SIZE          DENSITY      SIDED      CODE:NO      PRICE

     FIVE INCH      SINGLE       SINGLE     M11A411X       1.50
     FIVE INCH      DOUBLE       SINGLE     M13A411X       1.66
     FIVE INCH      DOUBLE       DOUBLE     M14A411X       1.82
     FIVE INCH      DOUBLE       SINGLE     M15A411X       1.50
     FIVE INCH      DOUBLE       DOUBLE     M16A411X       1.63
     EIGHT INCH     SINGLE       SINGLE     F11A211X       1.50
     EIGHT INCH     DOUBLE       SINGLE     F13A211X       1.84
     EIGHT INCH     SINGLE       DOUBLE     F12A211X       1.91
     EIGHT INCH     DOUBLE       DOUBLE     F14A211X       2.00

. REPLACE ALL PRICE WITH PRICE*1.1
00009 REPLACEMENT(S)
. REPORT FORM DISKPRICE

                    PRICE LIST FOR FIVE AND EIGHT INCH FLOPPY DISKS

        SIZE          DENSITY      SIDED      CODE:NO      PRICE

     FIVE INCH      SINGLE       SINGLE     M11A411X       1.65
     FIVE INCH      DOUBLE       SINGLE     M13A411X       1.82
     FIVE INCH      DOUBLE       DOUBLE     M14A411X       2.00
     FIVE INCH      DOUBLE       SINGLE     M15A411X       1.65
     FIVE INCH      DOUBLE       DOUBLE     M16A411X       1.79
     EIGHT INCH     SINGLE       SINGLE     F11A211X       1.65
     EIGHT INCH     DOUBLE       SINGLE     F13A211X       2.02
     EIGHT INCH     SINGLE       DOUBLE     F12A211X       2.10
     EIGHT INCH     DOUBLE       DOUBLE     F14A211X       2.20

. REPLACE FOR SIZE="EIGHT INCH" PRICE WITH PRICE+.10
00004 REPLACEMENT(S)
. REPORT FORM DISKPRICE

                    PRICE LIST FOR FIVE AND EIGHT INCH FLOPPY DISKS

        SIZE          DENSITY      SIDED      CODE:NO      PRICE

     FIVE INCH      SINGLE       SINGLE     M11A411X       1.65
     FIVE INCH      DOUBLE       SINGLE     M13A411X       1.82
     FIVE INCH      DOUBLE       DOUBLE     M14A411X       2.00
     FIVE INCH      DOUBLE       SINGLE     M15A411X       1.65
     FIVE INCH      DOUBLE       DOUBLE     M16A411X       1.79
     EIGHT INCH     SINGLE       SINGLE     F11A211X       1.75
     EIGHT INCH     DOUBLE       SINGLE     F13A211X       2.12
     EIGHT INCH     SINGLE       DOUBLE     F12A211X       2.20
     EIGHT INCH     DOUBLE       DOUBLE     F14A211X       2.30
```

Figure 5.11   Example of non-selective and selective transactions on record fields.

betic order on a field specified by an index file (DFIND) and then proceeds to clear the VDU screen, increase all the price fields in all records by 10 per cent and then display on the screen all those records whose resultant price field is greater than 10 and less than 100. To write a program in

```
DO MENU
                    DIRECTORY MAINTENANCE
                      *** MAIN   MENU ***

                    0 - LIST DIRECTORY
                    1 - ADD NEW RECORDS
                    2 - DELETE CURRENT RECORDS
                    3 - ALTER EXISTING RECORDS


                       WAITING INSTRUCTION


 WAITING 0

  00013   DAVISON G H          ACCOUNTS        721
  00017   WILLIAMS G S         ACCOUNTS        649
  00019   SMITH Y (MISS)       ACCOUNTS        407
  00006   LEWIS C D            INSPECTION      723
  00018   SMITH D H            INSPECTION      640
  00010   JAMESON F T          PERSONNEL       653
  00021   CHAMBERS J J         PERSONNEL       657
  00001   BROWN R G            PRODUCTION      345
  00014   ASHID T F            PRODUCTION      555
  00015   PIPER T F            PRODUCTION      921
  00016   SMITH F S            PRODUCTION      555
  00024   SINDEN D F           PRODUCTION      290
  00025   EVERSFIELD D S       PRODUCTION      555
  00009   RANKIN G H           PURCHASING      386
  00012   BROWNLY   A          PURCHASING      432
  00022   BOLT .. A            REGISTRY        412


 WAITING 1
  Enter 0 to exit


 Enter SURNAME I I:JAMES D F


 Enter DEPARTMENT:PERSONNEL

 Enter EXTENSION NO.:274


 Are all fields correct?:Y
```

Figure 5.12 Printout from a database macroprogram menu (operator's responses underlined).

```
WAITING 2
  Enter 0 to exit

      Enter 1 to delete a NAMED record
      Enter 2 to delete all records
      sharing a single EXTENSION number

WAITING 2
EXTENSION NUMBER to be deleted:555

00014  ASHID T F          PRODUCTION     555
00016  SMITH F S          PRODUCTION     555
00025  EVERSFIELD D S     PRODUCTION     555
DELETE?:Y

WAITING 3
  Enter 0 to exit

Enter SURNAME of persons
record to be changed:BROWN

These are all the records with that SURNAME
00001  BROWN R G          PRODUCTION     345
00012  BROWNLY G A        PURCHASING     432

Enter NUMBER of record
to be altered if MORE than one, OR
if ONLY one record listed, key in
that records number
:12

00012  BROWNLY G A        PURCHASING     432

Which FIELD do you want to alter
DEPARTMENT - D or EXTENSION - E?
WAITING E
New EXTENSION number:423

The new record is now as shown below


00012  BROWNLY G A        PURCHASING     423


WAITING 0

00013  DAVISON G H        ACCOUNTS       721
00017  WILLIAMS G S       ACCOUNTS       649
00019  SMITH Y (MISS)     ACCOUNTS       407
00006  LEWIS C D          INSPECTION     723
00018  SMITH D H          INSPECTION     640
00010  JAMESON F T        PERSONNEL      653
00021  CHAMBERS J J       PERSONNEL      657
00026  JAMES D F          PERSONNEL      274
00001  BROWN R G          PRODUCTION     345
00015  PIPER T F          PRODUCTION     921
00024  SINDEN D F         PRODUCTION     290
00009  RANKIN G H         PURCHASING     386
00012  BROWNLY G A        PURCHASING     423
00022  BOLTON A           REGISTRY       412
```

BASIC to achieve the same result would require perhaps 30 instructions as opposed to the four used here.

Figure 5.12 illustrates the type of database system that can be designed using a macro system. In this particular example, which is ranged to maintain a company's telephone extension list, the user is always referred back to a simple four-option menu which allows the user to:

0   list the directory,

1   add new records to the directory,

2   delete records from the directory,

3   alter existing records in the directory.

Throughout the example the operator's responses are underlined. The initial response, 0, produces a listing of the current records. The next reponse, 1, allows the user to add a record for a D. F. James who has joined the PERSONNEL department and has been allocated extension number 274.

To delete all the records associated with extension 555, the operator keys in '2' to access the delete records facility and a subsequent '2' to indicate it is records linked to an EXTENSION (rather than a NAMED person) that are to be deleted. The macroprogram then requests the EXTENSION NUMBER and, given the response 555, identifies all the records associated with that extention and deletes them when a confirmatory Y is keyed in by the operator.

To alter an existing record, the operator responds to the menu with 3 and inadvertently keys in BROWN rather than the surname required which is BROWNLY. Since that search criterion finds two records, the operator can identify the particular record required by keying in its number, 12. To reassure the operator, the selected record is displayed and the field to be changed requested. In this case the EXTENSION number is changed from 432 to 423 and the altered record displayed. A final response of 0 relists the directory and confirms that all the alterations/deletions/additions have been made correctly and that records have been kept in departmental alphabetic order.

The macroprogram to achieve this directory maintenance system consists of only some 60 instructions.

Conclusion

The facilities of database management and information retrieval packages illustrated in this chapter are typical of many such packages. Some do have fewer facilities; and only a few allow the user to write macroprograms where instructions like CREATE (create a file), SORT, APPEND, etc., can be used within a program in much the same way as the much simpler statements are used in a BASIC program. This macroprogramming facility offers exciting possibilities for management applications. However, they are normally the province of the professional systems analyst or programmer and only occasionally that of the enthusiastic manager.

Database management and information retrieval packages form the basis of many applications of microcomputers. The flexible type of proprietary package discussed here could be used far more widely were it not for the average user's preconceived fear that the design procedure involved is too complex. It is hoped that this chapter has, at least partially, dispelled that fear.

Before deciding to buy a flexible form of database management and information retrieval package, as opposed to a package tailored to a specific application consider the following:

is the application so specific as to require a bespoke system designed around a flexible package? For most stock control, sales/purchase ledger and payroll applications a specially designed, proprietary package is usually more appropriate;

are there further applications to which such a flexible package could be put to make it more cost effective?

More specifically:

can the data stored on records within a file remain confidential, i.e., is there a password control?

is the key field unique or non-unique? The former is preferable for efficiency, the latter if personnel records, etc., based on surnames are to be used;

can the number of records within a file be specified and is the maximum number of records per file acceptable for the particular application?

if a lot of information has to be stored per record, how many bytes (characters) per record can be stored, and how much information can sensibly be stored on the first screen before one has to resort to a multiple screen record?

is a report printing facility available and what range of facilities does it offer? To reduce the purchase price for users not requiring report printing, some packages are offered without a report generator facility.

Review of the more popular flexible database packages

Archive. This is the database component of the Integrated Business Package known as Xchange and, like the spreadsheet, graphics and word processing components, is available as a stand-alone package. Archive is a command driven package which like dBASE II/III can be used as a higher-level programming language. Archive uses a variable field length record structure and is therefore very economic in storage terms when saving database files on disk. A nice feature of the package is that loops and conditional statements included in high-level programs are automatically indented for ease of identification on the screen and when printed. Archive has a very simple and effective record screen design capability but does not have a report generator although, of course, one can be written for it as a macroprogram.

Cardbox. A relatively cheap, well-documented and easy to use package with standard rather than extensive database facilities. Its one particular advantage is that as maximum field lengths do not have to be specified in advance, it is a package which can very easily accommodate field contents which vary considerably such as text fields in library catalogue systems.

dBASE II/dBASE III. For long the market leader, dBASE II has been succeeded by the more expensive dBASE III whose main advantage is that it can cope with more than just two files simultaneously as in the case of dBASE II. Both packages are available on the IBM PC family and compatibles and also offer colour which is most useful when designing bespoke database systems for other users. In spite of its popularity dBASE II/III is not a user friendly package, being completely command driven. However, because of its command driven features, dBASE II/III is often used as a high-level database language by many programmer/consultants to design systems for their clients. Both packages have a sophisticated report generator but being fixed field length systems are not particularly economic in terms of storing database files on disk. dBASE III Plus is a multi-user version which only allows one user to access a particular record at one time.

DMS+ and Delta. Both these packages come from the same software house, with Delta offering the more comprehensive set of facilities at over double the price of DMS+.

DMS+ offers a fixed field/record length structure and although offering indexing facilities, index files have to be updated when new records are added or old records deleted. The package is menu driven with good report writing facilities and a letter writing facility. As with most menu driven packages the package is very easy for the novice to use but can appear somewhat cumbersome to the experienced user.

Delta has many of the facilities found in DMS+ but in addition allows multifile manipulations. Although it is not possible to use this package as a high-level database programming language, it is possible to save sets of control sequences which can perform as a bespoke system. This approach is not quite as flexible but is much easier to use.

Files and Folders. Designed specifically for use with the IBM PC, this package affects most controls through the use of the PC's ten function keys. The package operates on a fixed field/record length structure and up to eight files can be manipulated, three simultaneously.

FRIDAY. From the same stable as dBASE II/III, Friday is an attempt to produce a simple menu driven package for users not prepared to undergo the learning time required to operate its command driven stablemates. An easy to use, excellently documented package, it offers sufficient database facilities for standard record keeping.

Sensible Solution. Offers both menu and command driven methods of control. By imposing certain restrictions, such as no two fields in separate files having the same name, this package, by holding a central dictionary of the name and location of each field, makes it easy to relate sets of records.

6

Integrated business packages

When it was originally launched, Lotus 1-2-3 was hailed by microcomputer pundits as the first widely available 'integrated' package. However, this package (see page 86) for more details) was conceived essentially as a spreadsheet with added graphics and limited database facilities and, in retrospect, would now be regarded as a 'super' spreadsheet rather than as a truly integrated business package.

The concept of integration – advantages and disadvantages

As can be seen in figure 6.1, packages which now claim to be integrated business packages attempt in various ways to integrate the four principal microcomputer business functions or elements. These are word processing, spreadsheet, database and graphics to which some also add other facilities such as a personal diary, communications, terminal emulation plus file-transfer, etc.

Since it is generally agreed that the market response to integrated business packages has not been as ecstatic as their sponsoring software houses might have hoped and certainly has not matched the unit sales of 'super' spreadsheets, it might be sensible at this stage to detail some of the advantages and disadvantages of this form of business package.

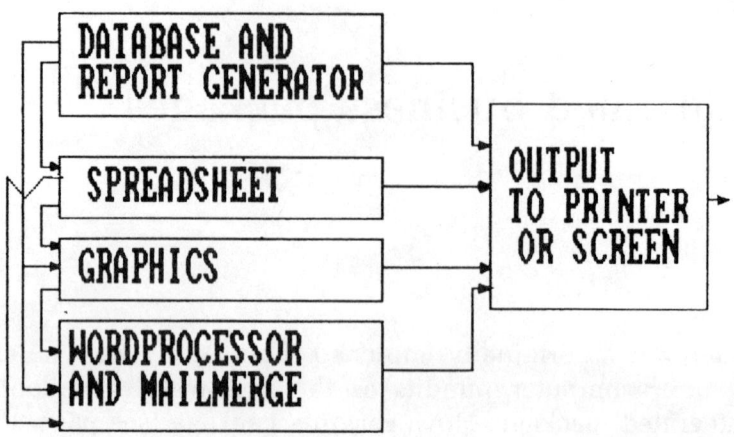

Figure 6.1 Linking word processing, spreadsheet, data-base and graphics within an integrated business package.

1   An integrated package which offers the four elements of word processing, spreadsheet, database and graphics will generally be cheaper than four separate, stand-alone packages offering these self-same facilities. However, integrated business packages are not that cheap and unless the potential user definitely requires all four elements, fewer stand-alone or separate packages can indeed be cheaper.

Integrated business packages which are 'disk based' (as opposed to RAM based) and achieve integration between the various elements via the medium of static disk files, can generally be purchased as several individual packages where each package represents one of the constituent elements. This package structure allows a user to purchase individual elements progressively although there is a cost advantage when all four are purchased simultaneously.

RAM based packages, which can only be purchased complete, do, however, have the advantage that they can display the output of more than one of the integrated elements simultaneously whereas 'disk based' packages can only display one at a time.

2 Although none of their originators would admit to the fact, integrated business packages are not easy to use and certainly the full potential of these packages can generally only be realized by attending a training course. The fact that such courses, with the necessary accommodation, can cost twice as much as the price of the package itself has certainly been one of the reasons that integrated packages have not proved to be as popular as many had hoped.

3 Because the programs required to perform all four elements within an integrated business package are collectively large, such packages may require a minimum of 512 kbytes of internal memory to operate satisfactorily and whilst most operate with a twin floppy disk drive format, some only operate with a minimum of 5 mbytes of hard-disk and are, therefore, not covered in this book.

4 One of the obvious advantages of an integrated package is that the screen format, command structure and documentation presented to the user can be made uniform (i.e., a common 'face' is presented). This standardization should make it much easier for the user to move between the various integrated elements and thus cut down the amount of learning required to use all elements for those users starting from scratch. However, a possible disadvantage of an integrated business package could be that the facilities offered by individual elements may not be as extensive as those contained within a specialized package concentrating on one element alone. Additionally, not all the elements within an integrated business package may be equally acceptable to an individual user.

5 Since integrated business packages were introduced to the market, and thus highlighted the assumed need of users to be able to integrate between different elements, several recently developed packages have now been produced which allow the simple transfer

of files between existing stand-alone packages. This alternative approach allows users to stay with their favourite packages whilst enjoying the benefit of a relatively high degree of integration.

Products such as GEM, Topview, The Integrator and Windows claim to fill this role.

6   Most integrated business packages, in addition to offering the four elements of word processing, spreadsheet, database and graphics, also offer communications and a macroprogramming facility with which relatively complex business systems can be designed. To take advantage of these facilities, a high level of programming ability on the part of the user is generally required. It is in this area – where third-party software houses are increasingly developing relatively complex business systems for their clients using the powerful facilities offered by an integrated business package – that many feel such packages are most suited.

Integration from a user's point of view

In discussing the potential use of an integrated package it might be most sensible to consider a possible business or management application which would involve all four elements of word processing, spreadsheet, database and graphics.

Of the four elements included in a typical integrated package, it is fairly clear that word processing is the element to which the other three would pass information whereas the word processing element would rarely be required to pass information to the other three. Additionally, transfers of information might also occur from the database element to either the spreadsheet or graphics elements and the spreadsheet element would certainly pass information to the graphics element, these two being now combined in most stand-alone spreadsheet packages.

A business application which might make use of all four elements could conceivably be:

a   A customer database which could provide information on numbers of customers by product type (using a report generator with subtotalling – see page 104) and additionally provide the information required for the mailmerging facility of the word processing element (see page 59).

b   Subtotal information on customer and product types passed to a spreadsheet for management to experiment with various marketing and sales strategies until a satisfactory strategy is evolved.

c   Information passed from the spreadsheet to the graphics element to produce bar or pie-charts of the chosen strategy.

d   Information (in the form of charts derived from the chosen strategy evolved using the spreadsheet fed with information from the database) passed from the graphics element to the word processor.

e   Word processor used to create final report and include charts passed from the graphics element. Supplementary information passed from both the database and spreadsheet elements to the word processor for inclusion in an Appendix of the report thus substantiating the charts included in the main section of the report.

This hypothetical process could appear in the way shown in figure 6.2.

Disk based and RAM based integrated business packages

Broadly speaking, integrated business packages can be divided into two categories, namely disk based and RAM (i.e., internal memory) based.

Disk based integrated packages such as Xchange,

APPLICATION OF AN INTEGRATED BUSINESS PACKAGE

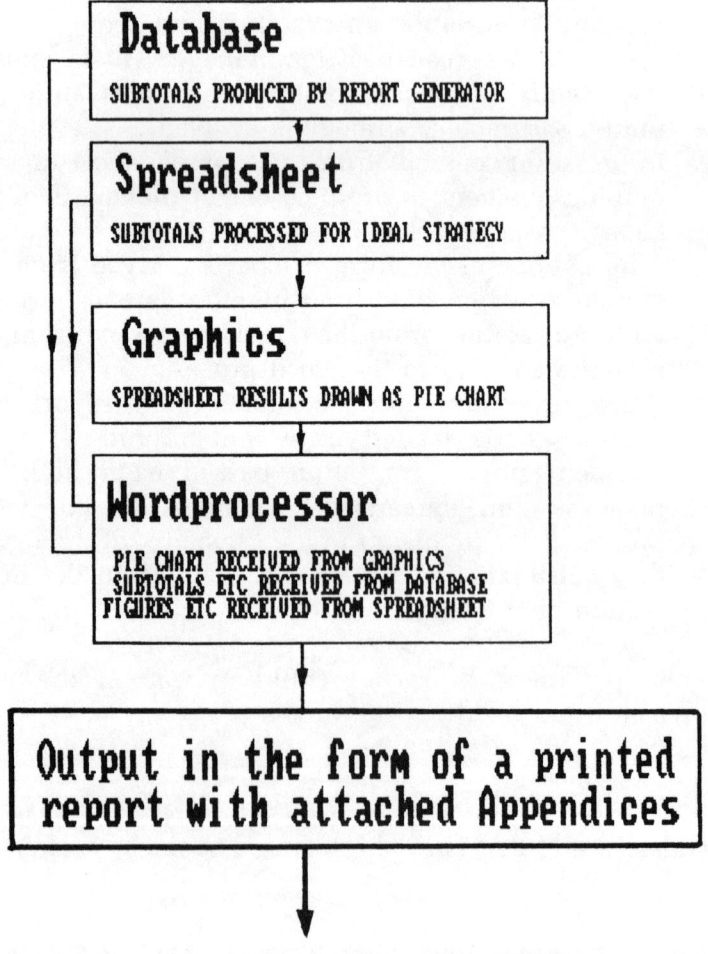

Figure 6.2   *Hypothetical business example using all four elements of an integrated business package.*

OpenAccess and Smart provide integration of the four computing elements of word processing, spreadsheet, database and graphics via the medium of disk files. Thus having developed, for example, a spreadsheet from which it is now required to produce a graph, the spreadsheet 'exports' a named file to disk in a form in which that file can then be 'imported' to the graphics element of the package.

This process is illustrated here using a popular disk based integrated package. In figure 6.3 a simple spreadsheet is about to be exported to disk – in a form acceptable to the associated graphics element of the integrated business package – as a file 'fcst'. Subsequently, in figure 6.4, this file 'fcst' has been imported from disk by the graphics element and displayed as a line graph which has been automatically scaled and provided with an interpretive key.

Disk based integrated packages, whilst much slower in operation than RAM based packages and unable to display

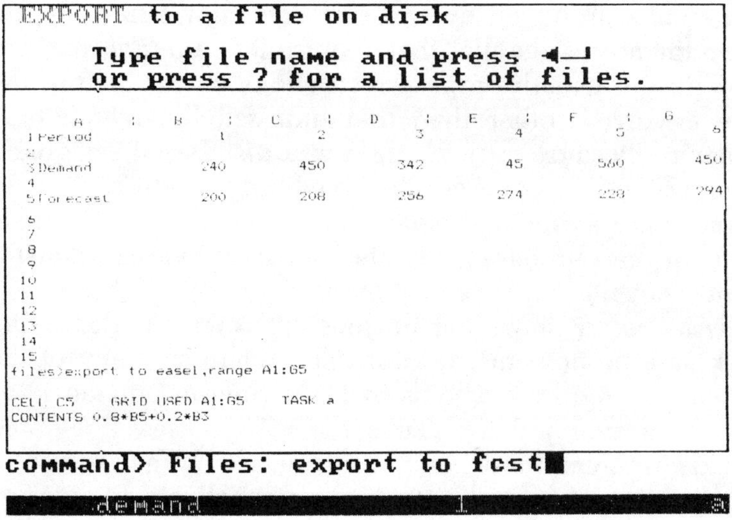

Figure 6.3 Simple spreadsheet about to be exported as a file 'fcst' for subsequent importing by the associated graphics element of a disk based integrated business package.

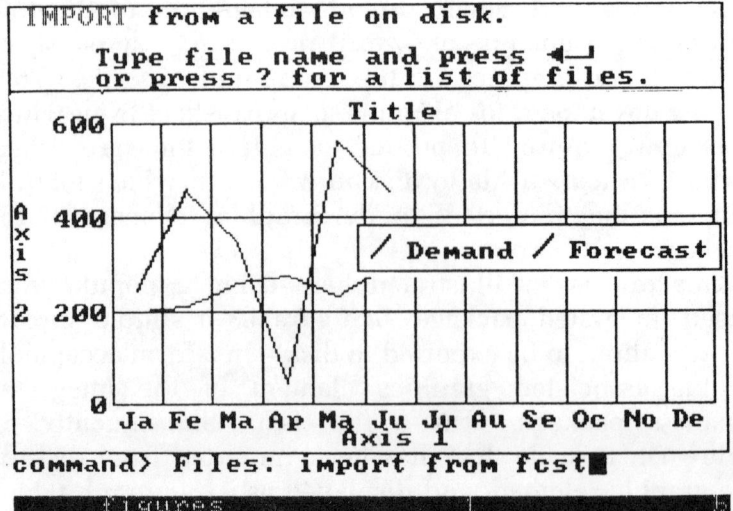

Figure 6.4   Graphics display of 'fcst' imported as a file from the spreadsheet element of a disk based integrated business package.

the results produced by two elements simultaneously, do have the advantage that they require less internal memory and do not usually impose restrictions on the size of the files involved, other than that imposed by overall disk capacity. Because each element of a disk based integrated business package uses the medium of disk files to communicate, such packages can generally 'stand alone' and can be purchased complete or as individual, constituent elements.

RAM based integrated business packages, whilst using disk as a permanent store for data, retain as many of the system's program elements in RAM (internal memory) as can be accommodated. Thus the RAM based integrated packages Symphony and Framework both require a minimum of 340 and 512 kbytes respectively of internal memory and offer greater operational speed than disk based packages. Another feature of such RAM based packages is that the results of two or more processes can be displayed simultaneously, whereas disk based systems can only usually display one at a time. However, since the provision of RAM is finite and is also required for operating system programs and data, the facilities offered within each individual element of such a RAM based integrated business package may be restricted relative to those which are disk based. In particular, the data associated with each application (often referred to as a window or frame) will often be limited in size, to 32 kbytes for instance. Whilst such windows or frames can be strung together for larger applications, such restrictions can be inconvenient, for word processing in particular.

However, the ability to display simultaneously the information derived from more than one element of an integrated package is a distinct advantage of the RAM based system, and the proponents of this type of package would argue that it represents the only form of true integration. This ability is demonstrated in figure 6.5 where the results of a simple spreadsheet are displayed simultaneously with its associated graph. Figure 6.6 takes this process one step further by demonstrating a RAM based integrated package's ability to display the results of more than two elements. In this example the spreadsheet

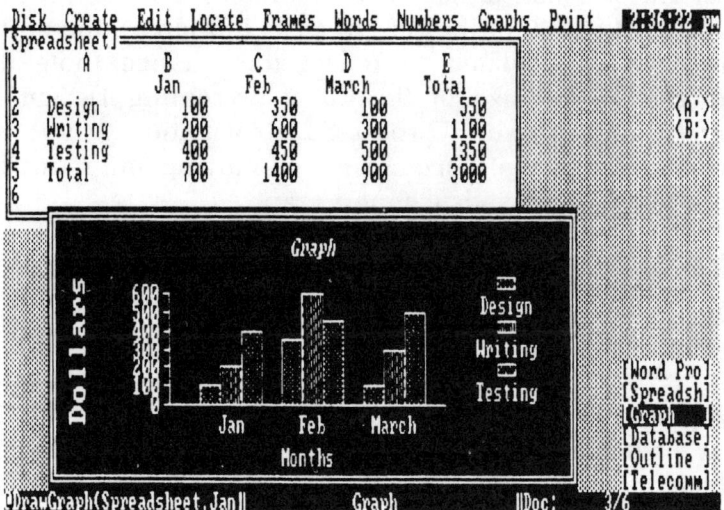

Figure 6.5   A simple spreadsheet and its associated graph displayed simultaneously using a RAM based integrated business package.

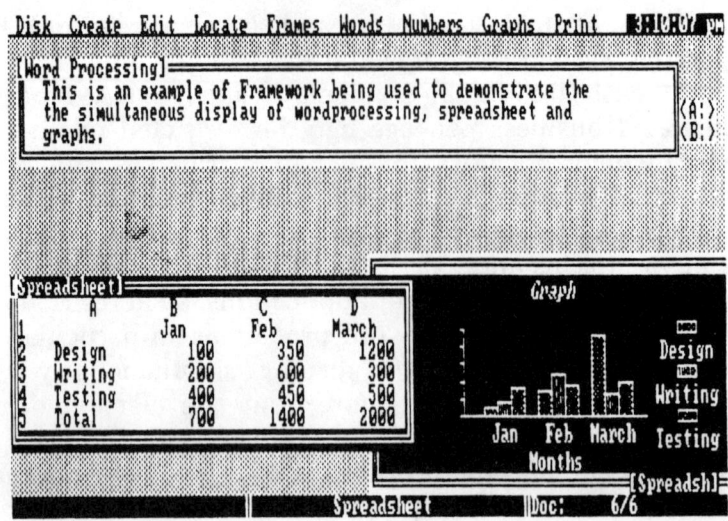

Figure 6.6 Modified spreadsheet and its associated, recalculated graph together with an additional word processed explanation.

and graph of figure 6.5 have been moved and reduced in size, the spreadsheet has been modified (note the increase from 100 to 1200 of the Design costs in March), the graph has been recalculated to reflect this change (note the increase in the size of the bar representing Design in March) and a word processed explanation has been incorporated in the space created by moving and reducing the size of the spreadsheet and graph.

Conclusion

Integrated business packages offer, in various forms, the four principal microcomputer functions required by the manager or business user. The four elements always offered within such integrated packages are word processing (for more detailed information on word processing see chapter 3), spreadsheet (chapter 4), database (chapter 5) and graphics.

Integrated packages can either be disk or RAM based, and each form has some relative advantages. Because they offer so many computing facilities, integrated business packages are not easy to use and attendance at a training course may well be necessary for the manager or business user to take full advantage of the facilities offered.

Review of the more popular integrated business packages

Electric Desk. Electric Desk is an unpretentious, relatively cheap but effective RAM based package. It offers the four basic elements required of an integrated business package together with elementary communications facilities. To utilize this package's facilities fully requires 512 kbytes of memory at which level nine smallish documents, spreadsheets and database files can be created and recalled with single key-strokes. Currently the cheapest integrated business package at approximately half the price of most of its competitors.

Framework. Framework is based on the concept of 'desktop', used as a working area onto which 'frames' – which appear as rectangular areas on the desktop – can be introduced. Individual frames are limited in size to the equivalent of 32 kbytes but a partial solution to this size limitation can be achieved by stringing frames together in an hierarchical structure since frames can contain further frames which can themselves contain other frames. Any changes to a constituent frame are reflected in frames further up the hierarchy. Individual frames can be 'zoomed' to full screen size and back again at will.

The word processing element of Framework offers a WYSIWYG (What You See Is What You Get) display. The spreadsheet and graphics elements are relatively standard and, as with most RAM driven integrated packages, spreadsheets and resulting graphs can be viewed simultaneously. As one would expect of a product from the same source as dBASE (see page 117) the database element of Framework is command driven and a powerful macro-programming language Fred offers impressive power and flexibility for application development.

Framework is generally regarded as being somewhat easier for the newcomer to use than its principal rival Symphony.

Logistix. Logistix is a RAM based package which requires 320 kbytes and operates in a similar fashion to Symphony. Somewhat cheaper than its rivals but more expensive than Electric Desk, this package offers an excellent colour spreadsheet together with basic text processing and a database facility based on records being represented by rows in the spreadsheet. Perhaps its most interesting feature is the 'timesheet' facility within which the user can define calendars, define jobs, enter start dates and esti-mated completion times and calculate the critical paths. Whilst obviously not as powerful as a dedicated project planning package (such as Pertmaster or Project Planner) this timesheet element is both unusual and useful.

OpenAccess. OpenAccess is a disk based integrated business package with a wide range of facilities. The database element is a powerful multifile program with screen design, validation and a query language. The spreadsheet element is of a reasonable standard and con-tains a goal searching facility which is unusual at this level. Goal searching allows the user to specify the required value of a dependent variable within a spread-sheet which then continually adjusts the value of a specified independent variable until the required value of the dependent variable is achieved. The word processing element is a WYSIWYG package with a limit of 32,000 characters per file which, when linked to the database element, can be used to mailmerge.

OpenAccess also includes a time management system (i.e., diary) which accepts booked in daily tasks and calendar events. It also includes autobooking and a searchable address file card index.

Smart. Smart is a disk based package and consists of three separate elements covering word processing, database and combined spreadsheet/graphics, each of which may be purchased separately. The system is provided with a main menu and integration is achieved through manual or automatic file swapping.

The word processing element is WYSIWYG and can be linked to the database for mailmerging. The database itself has multifile capabilities and can handle very large individual files. The graphics and spreadsheet are closely linked in a single element which overcomes the rather slow interchange between spreadsheet and graphics encountered in most disk based integrated systems. This is an important advantage when one considers that the majority of spreadsheet applications do generally require graphical interpretation. Eight different fonts can be incorporated into graphical displays and the size of the characters can also be defined. Smart includes an in-built programming language for designing system applications and also has a time management option.

Symphony. Symphony is a RAM based integrated business package owing much of its pedigree to Lotus 1-2-3. It claims to offer the largest spreadsheet currently on the market and its database facilities are modelled around the spreadsheet concept with each record being represented by a row within the spreadsheet. The limited display possibilities of this approach derived from 1-2-3 have now been overcome by providing a screen generation routine for record display. Whilst spreadsheets and resulting graphs can be viewed simultaneously, the initiation of subsequent graph printing is somewhat tedious as a separate printgraph module is required. The word processing element offers limited WYSIWYG presentation. A useful additional feature is a DOS access window which allows DOS commands to be invoked without leaving Symphony. Symphony offers a macroprogramming facility which makes it an attractive package for third-party software houses developing bespoke business systems. This latter feature has been one of the primary reasons for Symphony's market leadership in the integrated business package sector of the software market.

Xchange. Xchange is a disk based integrated business package comprising four stand-alone packages which can be purchased separately. With the exception of ARCHIVE (the database element) all packages are menu driven, the menus being removable from the display to increase the working area. The word processing element QUILL is a WYSIWYG package with virtually all the facilities expected of a good stand-alone word processing package including a mailmerge facility and the ability to recall sections of text such as addresses, letter terminations, etc., with a single key stroke. The spreadsheet ABACUS is remarkably versatile but tends to require complicated key sequences to achieve relatively simple tasks; it does offer prompts many of which are suitable and can be accepted simply by depressing the ENTER key. EASEL, the graphics package, offers the normal alternative graph/chart forms such as vertical and horizontal bar, stacked bar, line and pie-charts. It is one of the few graphics packages at this level which allows both bar and line representation in the same graph. Pseudo three-dimensional bar-charts are also available. ARCHIVE, the database element, is a command driven package with variable field and record lengths which offers a standard record display as a default; it also offers as an alternative a method of designing a display representation to suit the application being undertaken. ARCHIVE lacks a report generator but it is possible to create one using the commands as a programming language. As indicated already, integration between the four elements is performed via disk files and XCHANGE has the facility for returning the user to the processing position achieved earlier in the previously used element. A task sequencing language (TSL) can be used to configure application systems.

7

The microcomputer as a communications device

The majority of the business and management applications of microcomputers have so far been based on the microcomputer's power as an information processor. With the rapid improvements in methods of communication taking place, however, the microcomputer is now acquiring an increasingly important role as a communications device as well as an independent processor.

The theory of computer communications is technically complex requiring the synchronization of many elements, at hardware level, the operating system level and the applications software level. It is theoretically possible to link most computer based devices to most others, and this chapter touches briefly on the necessary technical requirements of communication. The chapter concentrates, however, on the two principal roles currently being acquired by microcomputers as a communications device within the business and commercial environment, namely:

micro to micro communications,

micro to mainframe communications.

Micro to micro communications – Local Area Networks

A Local Area Network or LAN allows from two to 200 microcomputers to be connected to each other for data communication purposes within a limited locality. Such LANs operate by physically connecting microcomputers to each other by a cable so that each computer within the network can then share:

information/data, or

a relatively expensive central resource such as a fast printer or large hard-disk facility.

Ideally a LAN manages the traffic between the various microcomputers and peripherals connected to the system whilst at the same time allowing each microcomputer to act as an independent processor. The distance over which microcomputers can be linked to each other on a local network without any signal boosting is usually about 1,000 ft but this can be extended up to about 5,000 ft if boosters are incorporated in the system.

In practice there are three basic LAN layouts:

bus – a single length of cable to which each micro (which can now be regarded as a station within the network) is connected. When a station wishes to send a message to another on the bus, it waits for the bus to be clear of other messages and then sends its message to the appropriate destination;

ring – a loop of cable to which all micros are attached. Messages travel around the loop in one direction only. Each station reads every message and recognizes those addressed to itself;

star – as the name suggests, this network configuration connects all machines or stations through a single central point, usually a microcomputer which acts as the file server or shared disk storage.

All LANs consist not only of the cable providing the physical link between machines but also:

in all but the simplest LANs, an individual plug-in card

or board enabling each microcomputer to be connected to the LAN;

a central host microcomputer controlling the network and usually providing the central hard-disk facilities required by the network to save the data files to be exchanged between stations connected to the system;

software mounted on both the central host and individual microcomputers.

A typical layout of a small LAN, in which a single IBM XT or AT is used as a central host and file server for a small network of several IBM PCs or compatibles sharing a printer, is shown in figure 7.1.

At the time of writing there are a multitude of local area network systems available on the market and even IBM are supporting two different systems, namely PC network and Tapestry. An added complication in choosing an appropriate system is that there are reportedly up to two dozen different network technologies in use.

The quality of a local area network depends on the services offered in terms of the management of the system. In very simple LAN systems microcomputers can be connected to the system through their standard RS232 port (thus obviating the cost of special plug-in boards) and allocated space on a single hard-disk (file server). In more complicated LAN systems, stations can gain access to the same files on a central file server and when conflicts arise – such as two users attempting to alter the same record in a database file – the management of the system has to be able to cope and allocate priorities.

In business and management situations, the motivation for investing in a local area network facility will depend on whether the benefits of shared facilities offset the costs of providing the facilities allowing that sharing to take place.

The costs involved in setting up a local area network will obviously depend on the size of the network and the facilities offered, but as a generalization it can cost between £800 and £1,200 per microcomputer connected.

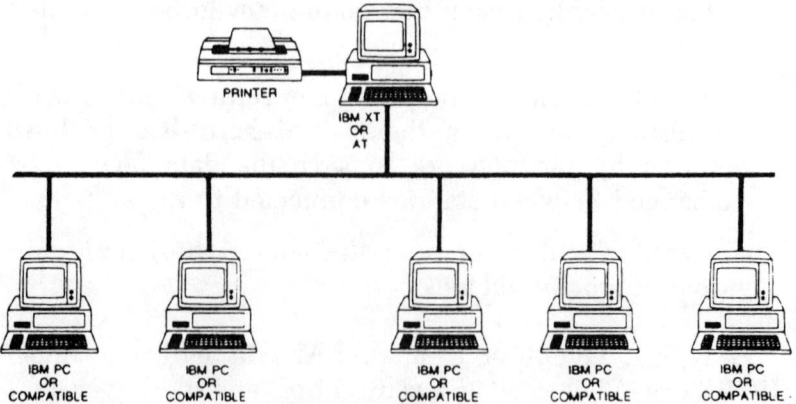

Figure 7.1 A simple LAN with an IBM XT or AT acting as a central host and file server for several IBM PCs or compatibles.

Additional costs will also be involved in providing a central host microcomputer – if one is not already available – and software for the central host. In practice, the minimum size of such a central host will be an IBM XT or equivalent.

Some of the principal benefits of incurring such costs, which have caused users to invest in LANs in business and management situations, are:

to allow several secretaries operating IBM PCs (or compatibles) as word processing stations, to share a relatively expensive printer, such as a fast laser printer costing in the order of £5,000;

to allow several users to share the facilities of common database files;

to allow several users to be connected to a local Electronic Mailing system (see page 139 for more details of non-localized Electronic Mailing systems).

Micro to mainframe communications

Ignoring the fact that a microcomputer can be made to operate as a 'dumb' terminal and be connected to an 'in-house' mainframe computer, the majority of micro to mainframe applications occur where a microcomputer is used to access a remote mainframe machine (often, in practice, a large mini) via a telephone system.

For a microcomputer to be connected to a telephone system, the digital signals of the computer have initially to be converted to sound signals which can be transmitted along normal telephone lines. The most common device used to achieve this signal conversion is known as a modem (for modulator/demodulator) and such a device must obviously be available at both ends of the commun-ication link, i.e., at the microcomputer and the mainframe. The modulator section of a modem converts digital signals from the computer into acoustic signals acceptable for transmission on the telephone network and the demodu-lator section converts acoustic signals received from the telephone system into digital signals acceptable to the computer. Modems operate at different speeds (known as baud rates) both in transmitting and receiving information and it is obviously necessary to ensure that the speeds set on the modem (usually by switches) and within the associated software match those of the system being accessed. The three most popular baud rates (i.e., evaluated as the number of characters transmitted per second multiplied by ten) are 300/300, 1200/75 and 1200/1200 – the two numbers in each case referring to the receive and transmit baud rates respectively.

Modems are relatively cheap devices ranging from £100 to about £400 at the top of the range. At the top level the best modems will autodial one of several previously stored numbers, recognize an engaged signal and keep retrying, and when eventually connected transmit an automatic log-in sequence. Some will even recognize the baud rate of an incoming call and respond accordingly.

Modems connect to the RS232 port of the micro-computer, which must be fitted with an asynchronous communications plug-in board, and through a jackplug to the telephone system's standard wall socket. Currently, a set of rules for controlling modems known as the Hayes protocol has become the *de facto* industry standard for these devices. Lotus 1-2-3, for instance, uses Hayes protocols within its communications facilities as do many other application packages. In purchasing a modem, therefore, it is now sensible to ensure that the equipment is Hayes compatible.

Modems are the most reliable method of connecting a microcomputer to the telephone system, but where such a 'hardwired' (i.e., direct) connection cannot be made it is possible to use the normal telephone handset as the connecting device in conjunction with an acoustic coupler which is provided with two rubber 'cups' designed to fit the microphone and earpiece or speaker of the hand-set. Acoustic couplers can be used wherever there is a normal telephone but they do cost more than modems and they are not quite as reliable, particularly over long distances. This slight lack of reliability is caused by the possible interference that can occur in the process of converting the digital signals from the computer to the acoustic signals required for transmission via the micro-phone, and converting the received acoustic signals into digital signals via the earpiece or speaker. Whether a modem or an acoustic coupler is used for connecting a microcomputer to a telephone system, an appropriate software package will also be required.

The cost of using a telephone system (such as British Telecom) to connect a microcomputer to a remote main-frame computer depends as in the case of ordinary speech based calls on the duration of the connection, the distance involved and the time of day at which the connection is made. However, most of the mainframe computer systems offering a service via British Telecom can be accessed by a local call.

Where the required mainframe computer is not located in the UK, however, an international service called Packet

Switch Stream (PSS) is available to avoid astronomic telephone bills for Europeans contacting the US. This service, which obviously charges, is a specialized form of telephone system specifically for computers. To use the system, a local telephone call connects the user to the nearest national PSS 'node' – an access point where the normal telephone system is connected to PSS. Once in communication with the node and having entered an acceptable personal code, the user enters the address number of the system required, and PSS then makes the necessary national connection, or IPSS in the case of an international connection. Because the PSS system is much faster and is more reliable than a direct phone call it does offer a very competitive service. It is also truly inter-national and allows connection to mainframe services anywhere in the world, particularly to the US where IPSS offers one of the few practical means of accessing the powerful dial-up computer services available there.

General dial-up systems in the UK

Mainframe computer services available to users via a dial-up connection in the UK offer two main services:

electronic mail, and/or telex

database information provision, or

a combination of both the above.

For the business user the major advantage of using an electronic mail service provided by a third party (as opposed to operating a system on the company's in-house machine) is that the user only pays rental, not the capital cost, and also avoids the long-term overhead costs of maintaining hardware, software and databases where provided. Additionally, if the user's organization operates at a number of geographically well-spread sites, it is easier and cheaper to dial into a large central system.

Some of the advantages of electronic mail for business purposes are:

speed of communication;

sender and receiver do not have to be available at the same time – as with normal telephone calls. This is particularly advantageous when communicating across many time zones;

costs of electronic mail systems can be very competitive compared with other forms of communication when using a micro as messages can be prepared 'off-line' using the micro's own word processing facilities and then transmitted very rapidly (in a matter of seconds).

There are four major dial-up systems offering electronic mail facilities in the UK:

Telecom Gold. This service is aimed squarely at the business user, its main facility being electronic mail. The system can be accessed via 300/300 baud 1200/75 baud and 1200/1200 baud as well as PSS. Gold is therefore readily accessible and, after rather a slow start, it is now relatively popular amongst the business community – so much so that at peak times the system's response time can be quite slow.

Users of Gold are divided into groups – usually based on companies subscribing to the system – with a 'manager' who has special facilities and is responsible for looking after the group's mailboxes. Each user of the system has a six-figure identification number, the first three figures being common to the group, together with a password access.

Outgoing telex facilities are also available on this system as is access to some of the major US database systems – thus it provides an alternative form of access to PSS/IPSS.

Prestel. This is essentially an information provision service and offers both graphics and colour on local access to 96 per cent of the UK telephone population. The system is based on 'pages' (i.e., a screenful of information) and the user is provided with page numbers (there are currently 330,000) as a means of identifying the information required.

Information on Prestel is supplied by 'Information Providers' (IPs) – usually companies or groups providing information about their specialized goods or services. A provider is allocated (and charged for) a certain number of pages and can make changes as and when required and can impose a charge for access to the information displayed on specified pages. If an access charge is imposed, the rate is displayed on the screen. The information provided by Prestel is very diverse and is very large in terms of pages and this can make it slightly difficult for the novice user to navigate the system efficiently. Some of the more important subjects available on the Prestel index are:

Air Travel, Air Lines, Airports, Assurance
Bank Services, Building Societies, Business Information
Car Hire, Career Advice, Colleges of Higher Education
Computing Services, Conference Facilities, Customs
Development Corporations, Education, Entertainment
Ferries, Financial Times Index, Government Information
Health & Safety, Holidays, Immigration, Information Services
Insurance, Law, Legal Advice, Mail Order, News
Package Tours, Pensions, Port Information, Rail Travel
Restaurants, Road Haulage, Road Maps, Teleshopping
Viewdata Services, Weather Forecasts, Zoos

In addition to public access areas – such as those indicated above – Prestel also provides pages which can only be accessed by authorized users. Prestel does offer electronic mail facilities but its predominant use is as an information provider.

Originally regarded as an expensive 'white elephant' Prestel recently announced that it had begun to make a profit on its day-to-day operations. This has been brought about mainly by the increasing use of Prestel in homes rather than offices. This increase in the home use of Prestel – now about 45 per cent of total subscriptions – results from the dropping of computer-connection charges outside business hours. Recently a 24-hour supermarket ordering system for food and groceries has been launched through Prestel which is available to subscribers in five London boroughs.

Easylink. Primarily a system geared to sending and receiving telex messages amongst the 1,600,000 telex users world-wide with the support of a back-up electronic mail service. The system's particular feature is that it can offer microcomputer users access to a well-established business communication system traditionally based on relatively expensive telex equipment.

Easylink is generally regarded as relatively cheap – particularly for the low volume user – and offers an efficient service in the restricted area of processing telex-style messages. It currently claims over 50,000 subscribers in the US and is pushing strongly for a greater foothold in the UK. Easylink offers users a cheap connection to the US telex system and it is even possible to send messages to recipients not connected to either Easy link or the telex system using a Mail-Gram service which guarantees next day delivery to the specified address. Easylink also offers a translation service to and from English and French, German, Spanish, Italian, Dutch, Portuguese, Danish, Swedish and Norwegian.

One-to-One. A relative newcomer to electronic mail, One-to-One claims to offer a wide range of facilities within a very user friendly environment. The facilities currently on offer from this organization are:

electronic mail-box with password security,

access to the world-wide telex system,

radio paging for urgent telexes or messages,

mailing list service to send messages to a pre-prepared list of customers or clients,

priority postal letter service to link with clients who are not subscribers to One-to-One,

courier letter service for personal delivery of documents.

Specialized dial-up database systems

A variety of interactive, specialized dial-up database systems are now available which can be of particular use to the business user.

The organizations offering these on-line database facilities, often referred to as 'vendors' or 'hosts', use large computer systems to offer subscribers access to a variety of specialized databases acquired in the form of magnetic tapes from organizations such as the financial and news press agencies, library cataloguing and abstracting services, etc., the so-called 'originators'. The longer-established of these originators, whose original principal business activity was often the production of hard-copy directories, abstracts, etc., discovered that the magnetic tapes that were a byproduct of their hardcopy production processes could also provide a valuable additional source of income when sold to vendors of dial-up, interactive database systems.

There are currently some 17 principal vendors or hosts of database systems, collectively offering on-line access to some 600 separate databases. It was reported in 1983 that 66 per cent of these vendors were located in the US, 22 per cent in the UK and that the majority of the remainder were based in Europe.

Some individual databases are available on several host systems and, confusingly, the rate of charging for access to the same database can vary significantly on different hosts. These costs can vary from £16 to £100 per hour on-line to the system and average around £25 per search when including telephone charges.

Those dial-up database systems located in the UK are always accessible via a local telephone call. The majority of the systems which are located in the US are accessible via PSS/IPSS although the largest vendors or hosts based in the US are now providing access to databases on computers located in the UK thus bypassing PSS/IPSS.

All database systems operate on the principle that the specialized information contained in individual databases is held in such an ordered way that users searching for specified information can eventually find it. Dial-up databases usually operate on a Key or Search String provided by the user which hopefully specifies the information required. A Key having been specified, the system then methodically searches its files to find information which matches the specification embodied in the Key or Search String. The choice of the Key or Search String is all important since too wide a specification can produce a superfluity of responses – sometimes at an inordinate cost. Some systems offer a cheap preliminary search for an item which produces a count of the number of occurrences of that item in each individual database held on the system; this preliminary search being, in effect, a loss leader service to encourage further more detailed searches at a higher cost.

For an untrained business user, most of these dial-up database systems can appear relatively complicated and user unfriendly and it is, therefore, often more cost effective for occasional enquirers to employ a specialist researcher – someone familiar with the particular idiosyncrasies of the host system – rather than try to get to grips with the system hierarchy themselves. Such specialists are generally familiar with a variety of systems and make a living by being able to extract the information required with a minimum of retries or searches – each of which incurs a cost. For business users who are prepared to do the work themselves, experience shows that most tend to stay with the same host, whose rules and systems they understand, rather than shop around different hosts to access the same database at a slightly cheaper rate.

Dial-up databases provide a useful service as they can store such large quantities of information and computer searching techniques are much faster and more sophisticated than alternative information retrieval methods. The rapid growth of this type of facility is clear evidence of this. The hardware and software costs of setting up effective database systems, to say nothing of the long-term costs of maintaining and updating them, are extremely high, however. Thus companies and organizations which are not in the information-gathering business are generally precluded from creating their own database systems for anything more than in-house information.

The costs of subscriptions to dial-up databases vary considerably, although the initial joining fees are generally nominal – usually only covering administrative costs, costs of brochures, etc. Having captured a customer, however, hosts/vendors generate their major income from database access (80–90 per cent of most search costs) to which must be added (from the user's point-of-view) the telephone/PSS costs of actually being connected to the on-line database system (10-20 per cent). A summary of the principal dial-up databases available in both the US and Europe and the databases to which they provide access is given at the end of the chapter.

Conclusion

The microcomputer is increasingly being used as a communications device. The technical difficulties of providing communication links between such devices continue to be overcome at reasonable costs. Micros can be linked to other micros in the locality using a LAN (Local Area Network) which allows for the sharing of facilities such as expensive peripherals (fast printers or large disk storage facilities) or information (either in the form of a common database or electronic mail). Micros can also be connected to mainframe computers (usually via a tele-phone network) and a variety of facilities of use to the business user made available from this source.

Review of the more popular dial-up databases

Host: Compuserve
Company: Compuserve Inc.
Country: US
Compuserve is a general database system with a business user bias. It offers databases covering information on agriculture, aviation, engineering, legal and medical sub-jects as well as a news service, financial, banking and travel information.

Host: Datasolve
Company: Thorn EMI
Country: UK
Datasolve's on-line dial-up database system is marketed specifically at executives wishing to pinpoint market facts via a telephone. Amongst the databases available on the system is one which includes 180 Mintel market intelli-gence reports. Access to newly released reports is immediate.

Another major database available through Datasolve is World Reporter – an international news archive which currently contains reports from *The Economist*, AP Newswire, the *Guardian*, the BBC's world news broadcasts and the BBC's external service news. World Reporter contains 150 million words supplied by 1,600 journalists and 212 bureaux to 15,000 organizations seven days a week.

Host: Datastar
Company: Information Industries Ltd

Country: Switzerland
This host offers mainly business information databases derived from such sources as International Economic Abstracts, Financial Times Company Information (FINTEL), *Harvard Business Review* and the *New York Times* information database.

Host: Dialog
Company: Lockheed
Country: US
Established in 1966, this host is the largest on-line database system with a collection of over 200 individual databases mainly used by professional researchers.

The data in Dialog consists mainly of abstracts from works published in hardcopy, magazines, book summaries and government papers and covers a vast range of topics. In general, the system provides references and lists of articles rather than raw information.

Particular databases provided by the system which are of interest to business users are:

PTS Annual Reports – in depth information on publicly held US and selected international companies;

Federal Index – information on US federal government agencies including verbatim reports of Congress;

Legal Resource Index – information derived from US law journals;

Economics Abstracts International – based on 1,800 journals;

Management Contents – based on 280 management journals;

PAIS International – covering public affairs information.

Another major database mounted not only on this host but also ORBIT and DATASTAR is ABI/INFORM which is based on 500 English language management and administrative journals and covers amongst other topics accountancy, auditing, banking, data processing, finance and telecommunications.

Personal users can access a substantial subset of Dialog out of peak hours at a third of the normal charge under the name of Knowledge Index (KI). When joining Knowledge Index from the UK the cost of PSS connection is included in the package.

Host: DOW Jones
Company: Wall Street Journal
Country: US

Dow Jones is mainly business oriented, offering in particular up to the minute details of the US stock market. It claims 250,000 subscribers and, as well as financial information, it holds a wide range of news stories collected from the *Wall Street Journal*, Barrons and directly from the Dow Jones news service.

Host: Finsbury Data
Company: Finsbury Data
Country: UK

Finsbury Data provides on-line access to its main database called Dataline whch principally holds company information. Dataline covers mainly European companies and provides financial information on nearly 3,000 companies from 17 countries. The majority of companies are from the UK and the US is excluded. Income statements, balance sheets, financing tables and accounting ratios are available for each of the companies. The information provided is detailed; in the case of income statements home and export sales would provide only two items out of a total of over 60.

Another database held by Finsbury Data is Textline which contains articles published in over 100 UK daily papers including some selected papers from Western Europe. Topics covered are companies, industries, economics, public affairs and EEC affairs.

Host: Infoline
Company: Pergamon International

Country: UK

This rapidly expanding on-line database system offers databases on such topics as chemicals, environmental protection, biology, biotechnology, geomechanics and health and safety.

Of principal interest to business users is the Jordanwatch database which provides basic company information on 950,000 UK active companies and 650,000 dissolved companies using as its source the UK Companies Registration Offices and the *London Gazette*. Jordanwatch also includes more detailed company accounting information on 25,000 selected UK companies covering profit/loss accounts, full balance sheets and asset details.

Other databases of interest are:

Dun & Bradstreet's Key British Enterprises – 20,000 British companies determined by annual turnover;

Patsearch – covering all utility patents issued by the US Patent and Tradesmark Office in all areas of technology.

Host: ORBIT
Company: SDC Information Services
Country: US

ORBIT claims to be the leading host for providing scientific and technical sources of information covering patents, chemistry, energy, engineering and government. ORBIT offers a multiple profile (i.e., search key) facility which can be used to perform crossfile searching and thus save time and connect costs compared with other dial-up systems.

Host: Scicon
Company: Scicon Ltd, BP Group
Country: UK

Scicon offers access to several databases, one of which is POLIS (Parliamentary On-Line Information Service) which was originally set up for Members of Parliament but which is now available to other users. It covers all forms of parliamentary proceedings but due to lack of use has discontinued the full text of Hansard.

Scicon also offers several other databases including:

ACOMPLINE – the database of the GLC library covering urban affairs and offering mainly an archive based service;

URBALINE – which keeps an updated daily listing index on current articles, journals and papers on the same subject;

the DHSS library catalogue – an index of books, papers and journals on health care, health planning and social service legislation.

Host: The Source
Company: Readers Digest Association
Country: US
This host offers facilities competitive with those of Compuserve including news, business and financial analysis and commodity and media information. A relatively easy system to use with menu drive search facilities.

Index

Abacus   87
acoustic coupler   138
address points   59
alphanumeric fields   91
AUTOEXEC.BAT file   30, 45
AVERAGE function   73

bar-chart   83
breakeven analysis example   79
buffered keys   57
built-in functions   73
business micros sold   16
byte   91

cardbox   117
cash flow analysis example   77
centring   55
character   91, 95
CLS   21, 32, 47
colour in spreadsheets   84
Compac   11
compatibles, list of   14
Compuserve   146
COPY   21, 32, 47
corrections   54
criteria for search   101

database
    packages, classification of   92
    terminology   91
Datasolve   146
Datastar   146
DATE   21, 32, 48
dBASE II, dBASE III   117
deletions   54
Delta   117

dial-up systems, UK   139
Dialog   147
DIR   21, 34, 48
DIR/W   34
disk based integrated packages
    123
disk drives   7
DISKCOPY   22, 39, 48
DMS+   117
DOS   19
    external command   38
    filenames   20
    formatting for   42
    internal command   20
    literature   19
    loading   28, 30
    National DOS disk transferring
        41
Dow Jones   148

Easel   87
Easylink   142
Easywriter II   65
editing and presentation   54
Electric Desk   129
ERASE   21, 36, 48
expansion slots   10

field
    alphanumeric   91
    numeric   91
file   92
    size of   95
filenames, DOS   20
Files and Folders   118
fill points   59

Finsbury Data 148
flexible database packages 89
forecasting analysis 80
FORMAT 22, 39
FORMAT/B 49
FORMAT/S 49
FORMAT/S/V 41
FORMAT/V 41
FORMAT/V 48
formatting
  a disk 40
  for DOS 42
formulae, replication of 70
forward referencing 85
Framework 129
FRIDAY 118

global record transactions 109
GRAPHICS 22, 45, 49
graphics in spreadsheets 82
greeting points 60

hard disk, caution relating to 42
headers 57
highlighting 55

IBM
  compatibles 6
  PC 4
  PC AT 7
  PC family 3
  PC Portable 5
  PC XT 6
indentation 57
indexing 98
Infoline 148
insertions 54
integrated business packages 119·
integration 122
internal commands 20
internal DOS command 32
internal memory 9
iteration control 85

justification 55

key 91
keyboard 8
KEYBUK 22, 45, 49

LAN (Local Area Network) 133

letter composing 63
line graph 84
line spacing 55
list of addresses, 60
Logistex 130
LOOKUP function 75
Lotus 1-2-3 86

macroprogramming 110
mailmerging 59
MAX function 73
merging files 58
microcomputer
  basic configuration 18
  as communications device 133
  communication with mainframe
    137
  communication with other
    micros 133
MIN function 75
modem 137
moving text 54
Multiplan 88

National DOS disk 23
NPV (net present value) 73
numeric field 91

Olivetti M24 12, 13
One-to-One 142
OpenAccess 130
operating systems 17
ORBIT 149

page
  controls 105
  numbering 57
  offset 57, 59
  width 55
paging 55
password access 98
PC–DOS/MS–DOS 17
Peachtext 65
pie-chart 83
Prestel 141
printer
  echo 36
  interface 9
printing fields 58
printing labels 65
proportional spacing 55

Quill   65

RAM based integrated business
    packages   123
record   92
  controls   105
  structure   94
  size of   95
RENAME   21, 37, 49
replace   54
replication of formulae   70
report
  designing   104
  example of   105
  writing   104

salutation field   60
Scicon   149
screen dumping   45
search criteria   101
Search/Find   54
searching for records   101
selective record transactions   109
Sensible Solution   118
simple database facilities   86
size restrictions   95
software   10
sorting   98
specialized dial-up databases   143
Spellbinder   65
spellchecking   65
spreadsheet
  concept   69
  examples   75
  packages   68
stationery   58

stock portfolio examples   75
subtotal controls   105
SUM function   73
Supercalc 3   87
Symphony   131
SYS   22, 45, 49

tabbing   57
Telecom Gold   140
The Source   150
TIME   22, 37, 49
TK!SOLVER   88
total controls   105
trailers   57
Trendtext/2   66
TYPE   22, 38, 49

underlining   55
using COPY CON: 45

Visicalc   88
VOL   22, 38, 50
volume name   41
Vuwriter   66

wildcards   31
'within record' calculations   96
Word   66
word processing   51
Wordcraft   67
Wordstar   67
WTDATIM   22, 44, 50
WYSIWYG   52

Xchange   132